D1377757

CARD NIGHT

CARD NIGHT

CLASSIC GAMES, CLASSIC DECKS AND THE HISTORY BEHIND THEM

52 GAMES

FOR ALL AGES

WILL ROYA

BLACK DOG
& LEVENTHAL
PUBLISHERS
NEW YORK

Black Dog & Leventhal Publishers
Hachette Book Group
1290 Avenue of the Americas
New York, NY 10104

www.hachettebookgroup.com
www.blackdogandleventhal.com

First Edition: July 2021

Black Dog & Leventhal Publishers is an imprint of Perseus Books, LLC, a subsidiary
of Hachette Book Group, Inc. The Black Dog & Leventhal Publishers name and logo
are trademarks of Hachette Book Group, Inc.

The publisher is not responsible for websites (or their content) that are not owned by
the publisher.

The Hachette Speakers Bureau provides a wide range of authors for speaking events.
To find out more, go to www.HachetteSpeakersBureau.com or call (866) 376-6591.

Print book interior design by Carlos Esparza.
Illustration credits can be found on page 233.
Additional text contributions by Richard Pot.

LCCN: 2020032707

ISBNs: 978-0-7624-7351-9 (hardcover); 978-0-7624-7352-6 (ebook)

Printed in China

APS

10 9 8 7 6 5 4 3 2 1

TO THE JACK OF SPADES.
YOU HAVE ALWAYS BEEN MY FAVORITE.

CONTENTS

I. CLASSIC GAMES

II. RUMMY GAMES

III. TRICK-TAKING GAMES

IV. GAMBLING AND CASINO GAMES

INTRODUCTION

Because we are all familiar with the modern deck of playing cards, a standard deck of Bicycle Rider Back playing cards seems very normal and traditional to most of us. But to people of the past, a deck like this is anything but normal! The reality is that playing cards have undergone a radical transformation since their first beginnings several centuries ago. Our modern playing cards evolved into a deck of fifty-two cards—with four suits in red and black and with two Jokers—by making a journey that took hundreds of years and involved traveling through many countries.

Let's survey the history of playing cards, paying close attention to the geographic influences that have helped to shape the modern playing card. Our whirlwind historical tour will begin in the East, under a cloud of uncertainty about the precise origin of playing cards. But from there we'll make our way to Europe, first to Italy and Spain, then east to Germany, then back west to France, and eventually across the channel to England. Finally, we'll travel over the ocean to the United States, where the United States Playing Card Company (USPCC) produces modern decks in the form that we now know them.

THE EAST

The precise origin of playing cards continues to be the subject of debate among scholars, and even the best theories rely more on speculation than proof. There is clear historical evidence that playing cards began to appear in Europe in the late 1300s and early 1400s, but how did they get there? They seem to have come from somewhere in the East and may have been imported to Europe by crusaders or tradesmen. The common consensus is that an early form of playing cards originated somewhere in Asia, and scholars have made links to cards in China, India, Korea, Persia, and Egypt, which may have eventually made their way to Europe. Some scholars believe that playing cards were invented in China during the

Tang dynasty, around the ninth century CE. There seems to be evidence of some kinds of rudimentary games involving playing cards (and drinking!) around this time. These early cards included icons representing coins, which also appear

as icons on playing cards that appear later in Western Europe. If the scholarship is correct, these early games played in the Tang dynasty would place the origins of playing cards before 1000 CE and suggest that playing cards originated alongside famous tile games like Dominoes and Mah-jongg, which were created around

Japan, 1700–1730

the same time. Some have suggested that playing cards first functioned as play money and represented the stakes used for gambling games, and later they became part of the games themselves.

We cannot be totally sure that playing cards first appeared in the East, though evidence strongly suggests that is the case. Let's head to Europe and the earliest confirmed reference to playing cards, which is found in a Latin manuscript written by a German monk living in a Swiss monastery.

ITALY AND SPAIN

In a manuscript dated 1377, German monk Johannes from Switzerland mentions the appearance of playing cards and names several different card games that could be played with them. In the 1400s, playing cards often appeared along with dice games in religious sermons as examples of gambling activities that were denounced, and there is clear evidence that a fifty-two-card deck existed and was used during this time. The suits in the first European decks of the fourteenth century were swords, clubs, cups, and coins, and they very likely had their origin in Italy, although some connect these early suits with the cups, coins, swords, and polo sticks found on Egyptian playing cards from the Mamluk period. At any rate, these are the four suits still found in Italian and

Spanish playing cards today, and they are sometimes referred to as the Latin suits.

The court cards from late-fourteenth-century Italian decks typically included a mounted King, a seated and crowned Queen, plus a Knave. The Knave is a royal servant, although the character on the card could also represent a prince and would later be called a Jack to avoid confusion with the King. Spanish cards developed somewhat differently, with the court cards depicting a King, a Knight, and a Knave, with no Queens represented. The Spanish packs also didn't have a 10, and with the absence of 8s and 9s in the national Spanish card game known as Ombre, the typical Spanish deck usually only included forty cards.

The first playing cards in Italy were beautiful, hand-painted luxury items found only among the upper classes. But as card playing became more popular, and methods were developed to produce them more cheaply, playing cards became more widely available. It was only natural that this new product eventually spread west and north, and the next major development in playing card history occurred as a result of their reception in Germany. One historian has described their rapid spread as "an invasion of playing cards," with soldiers also assisting in their movement across the continent.

GERMANY

To establish themselves as a card-manufacturing nation in their own right, the Germans introduced their own suits to replace those created by the Italians, and these new suits reflected the German interest in rural life: acorns, leaves, hearts, and bells; the latter being hawk bells and a reference to the popular rural pursuit of falconry. The Queen was also eliminated from the German court cards, which instead consisted of a King and two Knaves, an obermann (upper) and untermann (under). Meanwhile, the 2 replaced the Ace as the highest card, to create a forty-eight-card deck.

Custom decks abounded, and suit symbols used in the novelty playing cards from this era include animals, kitchen utensils, and appliances, from frying pans to printers' inkpads. The standard German suits of acorns, leaves, hearts, and bells were predominant, however, although in nearby Switzerland it was common to see a variation using flowers instead of leaves, and shields instead of hearts. The Germanic suits are still used in parts of Europe today and are indebted to this period of history.

But the real contribution of Germany was their methods of printing playing cards. Using techniques of woodcutting and engraving in wood and copper that were developed as a result of the demand for holy pictures and icons, printers were able to produce playing cards in larger quantities. This led to

Germany gaining a dominant role in the playing card trade. Eventually, the new suit symbols adopted by the Germans became even more common throughout Europe than the original Italian ones.

Germany, 1850

FRANCE

Meanwhile, early in the fifteenth century, the French developed the icons for the four suits that we commonly use today: hearts, spades, diamonds, and clubs, although they were called coeurs, piques, carreaux, and trefles, respectively. It is possible that the clubs (trefles) derive from the acorns and the spades (piques) from the leaves of the German playing cards, but they may also have developed independently. The French also preferred a King, Queen, and Knave as their court cards.

But the real stroke of genius that the French came up with was dividing the four suits into two colors: red and black. Also, using clearer, simplified symbols meant that playing cards could be produced with stencils a hundred times more quickly than using the traditional techniques of woodcutting and engraving. With improved processes in manufacturing and the development of better printing procedures, including Gutenberg's printing press (1440), the slower and more costly traditional woodcut techniques were replaced with a much more efficient production system. For sheer practical reasons, the Germans lost their earlier dominance in the playing card market as the French decks and their suits spread all over Europe, giving us the card designs that we still use today. Still, it was only when playing cards emigrated to

France, 1745

England that a common design really began to dominate the playing card industry.

ENGLAND

Our journey across the channel actually begins in Belgium, which began exporting massive quantities of cards to England, although soldiers from France may also have helped introduce playing cards to England. Due to heavy taxes in France, some influential card makers emigrated to Belgium, and several card factories and workshops began to appear there. Rouen in particular was an important center of the printing trade. Thousands of decks of Belgian-made playing cards were exported to countries throughout Europe, including England. In view of this, it is no surprise that English card players have virtually always been using the French designs.

But playing cards did not pass through Europe without the English leaving their stamp on them. To begin with, they opted to use the names *hearts*, *spades*, *diamonds*, and *clubs* to refer to the suits that the French had designated as *coeurs*, *piques*, *carreaux*, and *trefles*. It is also to the English that we owe the place of honor given to the Ace of spades, which has its roots in taxation laws. The English government passed an act stating that cards could not leave the factory until they had proof that the required tax on all playing cards had been paid. This initially involved hand stamping the Ace of spades, probably because it was the top card in each deck. But to prevent tax evasion, in 1828 it was decided that going forward the Ace of spades had to be purchased from the Commissioners for Stamp Duties, and that it had to be specially printed along with the manufacturer's name and the amount of duty paid. As a result, the Ace of spades card tended to feature elaborate designs along with the manufacturer's name. Only in 1862 were approved manufacturers finally allowed to print their own Ace of spades, but the practice of an ornate Ace with the manufacturer's name was often continued. To this day, it is the one card in a deck that typically gets special treatment and elaborate designs.

The artwork on English court cards appears to have been largely influenced by designs produced in Rouen, which produced large numbers of playing cards for export. They include details such as Kings with crowns, flowing robes, beards, and longish hair; Queens holding flowers and scepters; and Knaves that are clean-shaven, wearing caps, and holding arrows, feathers, or pikes. It was also around this time that double-ended court cards became common (to avoid the need to turn the cards, thereby revealing to your opponent that you had court cards in your hand), and the existing full-length designs were adapted to make them double-ended.

England, 1770

UNITED STATES

The Americans are late companions on our historical journey, because for a long time they simply relied on imports from England to meet the demand for playing cards. Due to the general public's preference for goods of English origin, some early American card makers even printed the word *London* on their Ace of spades, to ensure commercial success.

One major innovation that we owe to the United States is the addition of the Jokers to the standard card deck. The Joker was initially referred to as "the best bower," which is terminology that originates in the popular trick-taking game of Euchre and refers to the highest trump card. It is an innovation from around 1860 that designated a trump card that beat both the otherwise highest-ranking right bower and left bower. The word *euchre* may even be an early ancestor of the word *Joker*. A variation of poker around 1875 is the first recorded instance of the Joker being used as a wild card.

Besides these small changes, America has not contributed any permanent additions to the standard deck of cards, which already enjoy a long and storied history and have become more and more standardized. However, the United States has become important in producing playing cards. Besides the previously-mentioned companies, other well-known names of printers from the late nineteenth century include Samuel Hart and Co. as well as Russell, Morgan and Co., the latter eventually becoming today's industry giant: the United States

Playing Card Company. American manufacturers have been printing special-purpose packs and highly customized decks of playing cards throughout their history, but the USPCC's Bicycle, Bee, and Tally-Ho brands have become playing card icons.

The history of playing cards is long and fascinating. What will the future hold for the fate of the humble playing card, and what will be the lasting contribution of our own era to the shape and content of a standard deck? Only time will tell. Meanwhile, you can enjoy a modern deck, knowing that it has striking similarities with the playing cards of fifteenth-century Europe, and that playing cards have been an integral part of life and leisure across the globe for more than six hundred years.

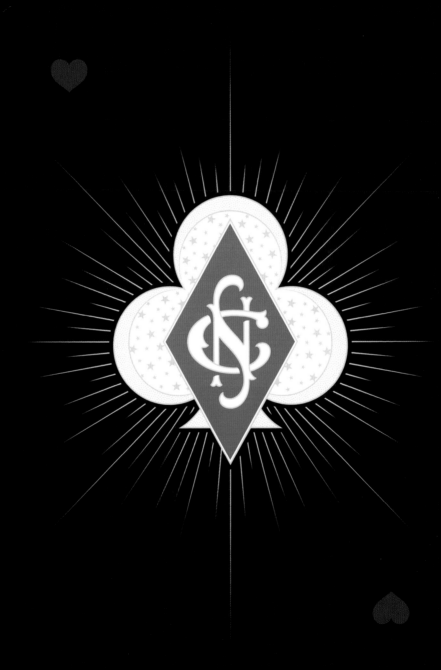

CLASSIC GAMES

Almost as soon as playing cards were invented, they became a popular way to have fun and pass the time. No matter how old you are or where you're from, you can always enjoy a good game of cards, either by yourself or with your friends and family.

BINGO

Bingo is a classic card game for four or more players of any age. Bingo uses two standard decks of fifty-two playing cards. More decks can be used, depending on the number of players and the amount of space available.

SETUP

Before gameplay can begin, a caller must be selected. Each player draws a random card from a shuffled deck. The player with the lowest card becomes the caller. Ties are broken with repeated drawings. The caller shuffles both decks and then deals five cards, face up, to each player (players can opt to have additional groups of five cards to make the game more like regular Bingo). The remaining cards in the deck stay with the caller.

HOW TO PLAY

The caller then draws cards from the shuffled deck and announces the rank and suit. If a player has that card in their hand, they flip it face down on the table. When a player's cards are all face down, they shout "Bingo!" and win the round.

CRAZY EIGHTS

Crazy Eights is a classic game for two or more players of all ages. It is played with a standard deck of fifty-two playing cards. The objective is to earn the fewest points. Once any player reaches 100 points or more, the game ends and the player with the lowest number of points wins.

SETUP

Before gameplay can begin, a dealer must be selected. Each player draws one card from a shuffled deck. The player with the lowest card becomes the dealer. The dealer shuffles the deck and deals five cards, face down and one at a time, to each player. The remaining cards form the stock and are placed in the center of the group. The top card from the stock is flipped over and placed next to the stock. This will form the discard pile. If the first card is an 8, the 8 is placed somewhere in the middle of the stock and a new starter card is flipped over.

HOW TO PLAY

Starting with the person to the left of the dealer, players try to get rid of their cards by placing them on top of the flipped-up card in the center. Players may do so if the card they want to get rid of is the same rank or the same suit as the card on top of the discard pile. Eights are wild, and if a player plays an 8, they must state what suit the 8 will be for the next player.

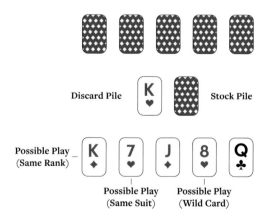

If a player cannot place any of their cards on the top card of the discard pile, they must draw cards from the stock until they can do so or they've drawn a maximum of five cards.

SCORING

After a player gets rid of all of their cards, the round is over and points are tallied. Cards remaining in players' hands are counted based on the following point values:

Card Type	Value
Ace	1 point
2 through 9 (except the 8)	Points correspond to face value
10, Jack, Queen, King	10 points
8	50 points

Once any player reaches 100 points or more, gameplay ends and the points are tallied. The player with the lowest number of points is the winner.

CRIBBAGE

Cribbage is a two-person card game played with a standard deck of fifty-two playing cards. It is a fairly complex game that is best suited for players of advanced skill. The objective of Cribbage is to be the first player to reach 121 points (or 61 points, depending on the version you're playing). Cards are ranked with Kings high and Aces low. Each numbered card is worth its own value, face cards are worth 10 points, and Aces are worth 1. Unlike other card games, Cribbage is scored on a wooden board with pegs.

SETUP

Each player receives three pegs, which are placed at 0 on the Cribbage board. To decide who becomes the first dealer, the deck is shuffled and then each player selects a random card. The player who draws the lowest-value card becomes the first dealer. The dealer then deals six cards, face down, to each player. Players review their cards and then choose two cards to remove from their hand. These cards are combined and set aside, face down, to form a "crib."

HOW TO PLAY

Typically, players move two pegs, leapfrogging one in front of the other, around the cribbage board to keep track of the points they earn during play. The third peg can be used to keep track of the number of games each player has won. Players are only able to move their pegs forward on the board by scoring points, which are awarded in the three rounds: pegging, counting, and crib.

PEGGING. In the pegging round, players score points by taking turns laying down their cards. After the crib is formed, the non-dealer shuffles the remaining cards and selects one card randomly, turning it face up. This card is referred to as the starter and is used to help calculate points at the end of play. The starter card is placed to the side as play begins.

Next, the non-dealer plays one card from their hand in front of them (each player's cards are kept separate). The dealer then plays a card against that card, and so on, until both players are out of cards.

As each person lays down a card, they must announce the running numerical total of the cards that have been played. For instance, if the non-dealer begins with a 7, they must say "Seven" as they lay down their card. If the dealer then lays down a 9, they must say "Sixteen" as they lay down their card, and so on until players reach 31 points total. Once players reach 31 points, the running total reverts to 0 and play continues until each player has played all four cards, at which time points are awarded.

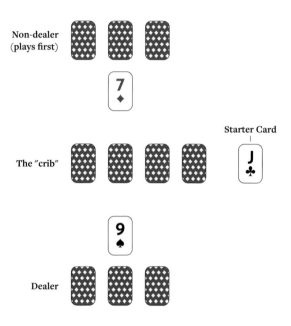

In the pegging round, the starter card that was drawn at the beginning of play may be used to help both players earn points in the counting round. Points are awarded in the following ways:

- As players continue to announce the running total of cards laid down, they may never exceed a total of 31. If a player reaches 31 exactly, they receive 2 points.

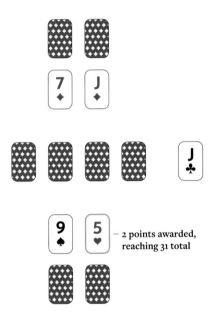

2 points awarded, reaching 31 total

- If a player makes a pair with the card just played, they receive 2 points. If a player makes a three of a kind with the last two cards played, they receive 6 points, and if they make four of a kind with the last three cards played, it is worth 12 points.

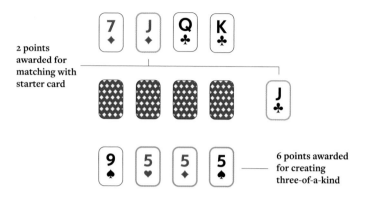

2 points awarded for matching with starter card

6 points awarded for creating three-of-a-kind

- A run of three or more played cards is worth the total number of cards included in the run. For example, a run of a 2, a 3, a 4, and a 5 is worth 4 points.
- If, at any time during play, a player cannot lay down a card to create a 31 count or less, that player must say "Go," and their opponent receives 1 point. The opponent continues gameplay if possible, otherwise a new round starts with the player who was unable to play a card.
- Playing the last card of the hand is worth 1 point.
- If either player has any two cards in their hand (including the starter card) that add up to 15, that player scores 2 points.
- If the randomly selected starter card is a Jack, the dealer earns 1 point.

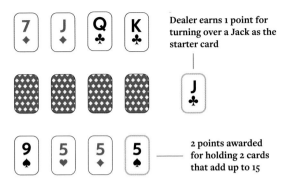

Dealer earns 1 point for turning over a Jack as the starter card

2 points awarded for holding 2 cards that add up to 15

COUNTING. In the counting round, players score points by making combinations with their existing hand and the randomly selected starter card from the pegging round. The non-dealer goes first in the counting round.

In the counting round, points are awarded in the following ways:

- Each unique combination that adds up to 15 is worth 2 points. This rule applies in both the pegging round (above) and this counting round.
- A run of three or more cards is worth the total number of cards that are included in the run.
- If a player has a pair, they receive 2 points. Three of a kind is worth 6 points, and four of a kind is worth 12 points.
- A four-card flush is worth 4 points; a five-card flush is worth 5 points.

- Having a Jack of the same suit as the randomly selected card is known as a nob. Nobs are worth 1 point.

CRIB. As mentioned before, the two cards discarded by each player at the beginning of each round form the crib. In the crib round, only the dealer is able to access the cards in the crib, and the dealer may use the cards from the crib to earn more points as laid out in the pegging and counting rounds above. The crib hand may not be combined with a player's original hand. The crib hand may only be combined with the starter card.

After the pegging, counting, and crib rounds are completed, the dealer position rotates, the deck is shuffled, new cards are given, a new random card is selected, and the rounds begin again. The first player to reach 121 points (or 61 points, depending on the version) wins the game.

VARIATIONS

KINGS CRIBBAGE. Invented by Cococo Games, Kings Cribbage is much like a combination between Cribbage and Scrabble. To begin, two to four players select five tiles from a bag of 104 tiles. The tiles are marked with symbols that represent the fourteen card types (Ace, 2, 3, and so on, all the way through King and the Joker). Players then take turns laying down one to five tiles on a Scrabble-like board in hopes of winning points. Points are given by making the same combinations one would make in a classic game of Cribbage. For example, laying down three King tiles would be the same as making a three of a kind combination in Cribbage. The Cribbage point values are the same in Kings Cribbage as well. For example, a four-card flush is worth 4 points.

CRIBBAGE SOLITAIRE. Cribbage Solitaire, as the name might suggest, is a one-player version of Cribbage. To start, two six-card hands are dealt. Then two cards from each hand are discarded to form the crib. A starter card is selected at random from the remaining deck. Regular play then proceeds based on the rules for basic Cribbage, but with a single player overseeing both hands. The player's goal is to reach 121 points.

HISTORY OF CRIBBAGE

Cribbage was created by the poet John Suckling in the seventeenth century. Suckling developed Cribbage from the now rarely played game of Noddy, which was invented around

the late sixteenth century. The lasting power of Cribbage is undoubtedly due to the fact that since the 1600s, the rules of the game have remained basically the same. The only major change in the game has been the adoption of an initial six-card hand instead of a five-card hand, although most Cribbage players in the UK still adhere to the classic five-card version of the game.

In addition to a stability in rules, Cribbage has remained a popular game throughout the centuries thanks in part to the Victorian novelist Charles Dickens. Dickens famously depicted the game in his classic novel *The Old Curiosity Shop*. Dickens also featured the game Beggar My Neighbor (see page 20) in *Great Expectations*.

DEVIL'S GRIP

Devil's Grip is a grid version of classic Solitaire. This single-player game is played with two standard decks of fifty-two playing cards with the Aces removed, for a total of ninety-six cards. The objective of the game is to build up piles in sequences and to limit the number of cards in your stock.

SETUP

After you remove all of the Aces in your two decks, shuffle the cards and build a grid of eight columns with three cards in each column. All of your cards should be facing up. The remaining cards form the stock and are placed face down at the bottom of the grid.

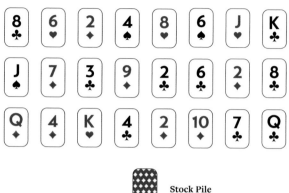

Stock Pile

HOW TO PLAY

The object of this game is to get rid of cards from the stock by building up piles of cards in a specific sequence. The goal is to have each of the eight piles in the first row stacked in sequences of 2, 5, 8, and Jack, with each sequence formed by four cards of the same suit. In the second row, each pile should be stacked in the order of 3, 6, 9, and Queen, and once again each sequence should be formed using cards of the same suit. Finally, in the third row, each pile should be stacked in the order of 4, 7, 10, and King of the same suit.

This order may seem strange, but it makes sense when you see the order laid out in the final grid. When the game is complete, you should have a three-by-eight grid of cards that looks like this:

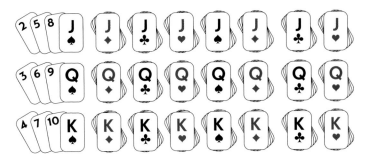

You can switch cards around to get them in position to start building piles.

If you move a card in the grid to build on a pile, the top card of the stock fills the gap in the grid.

If you cannot move any of the cards in the grid, cards from the stock can be dealt in sets of three. You may only use the top card showing. If all of your stock has been dealt, the dealt cards are flipped over to form a new stock.

When no more moves can be played, the game is over and points are tallied.

SCORING. The number of cards you have left in your stock corresponds to the number of points you have earned. Face cards are worth 10 points. For instance, if you end a game with a 9 of diamonds and a Jack of hearts in your stock, you've earned 19 points. The closer your score is to 0, the better. And be forewarned: It is exceedingly difficult (and exceedingly rare) to achieve a score of 0.

EGYPTIAN RAT SCREW

Egyptian Rat Screw is a fast-paced, multiple-player game (two to five players is best) that combines chance with agility. It is played with a standard deck of fifty-two playing cards, and the objective of the game is to take possession of all of the cards in the deck through drawing and slapping. This game is especially popular with school-age children and is a summer camp classic.

SETUP

Before gameplay can begin, a dealer must be selected. Each player draws one card from a shuffled deck. The player with the lowest card becomes the dealer. The dealer shuffles the deck and deals all of the cards one at a time to each player, going clockwise. Players may not look at the cards they have been dealt. It is okay for some players to have more cards than others at the game's outset.

HOW TO PLAY

Starting with the player to the left of the dealer and moving clockwise, players take turns drawing the top card of their deck and placing it face up in a pile in the center of the group. Players must draw cards away from themselves and toward the center of the table so that all players can see the card's value at the same time.

Players can win all of the cards in the pile and advance in the game via two different methods: face cards and slapping. Whenever a player picks up a pile of cards, the cards must be added to the bottom of the player's hand and they may not be shuffled.

FACE CARDS. If a player draws an Ace or a face card from their deck, the next player has a given number of chances to also turn up an Ace or a face card; if they cannot, the pile goes to the player on their right. A player's number of chances to draw an Ace or a face card depends on which card was initially drawn:

- If an Ace is drawn, the next player has four chances to turn over an Ace or a face card.
- If a King is drawn, the next player has three chances.
- If a Queen is drawn, the next player has two chances.
- If a Jack is drawn, the next player has one chance.
- Whoever wins the pile of cards must play the top card of their deck to restart play.

SLAPPING. When any of the following card combinations occur during gameplay, players must slap the pile immediately. Whoever gets their hand down first wins all of the cards in the pile and must then flip over the top card in their hand to restart play:

- Two cards of the same rank are played consecutively.
- The card played is the same rank as the first card of the pile (e.g., one 7 on top of another 7).
- Any combination of King and Queen are played consecutively.
- The number value of the cards played adds up to ten.
- An ascending or descending run of four cards is played.

PENALTY. If a player slaps the pile when no combinations are in effect, they must add two cards to the bottom of the pile.

VARIATION

BEGGAR MY NEIGHBOR. Beggar My Neighbor is a simple card game for two players. Each player receives twenty-six cards from a shuffled deck.

Gameplay begins when one player flips over the top card from their pile and places it in the middle of the playing area. If the card is not an Ace or face card, the other player flips over their top card.

Drawing continues until someone flips over an Ace or face card. When that happens, the next player has a number of chances to also flip over an Ace or face card:

If the card played is an Ace, the next player has four chances.

If the card is a King, the player has three chances.

If the card is a Queen, the player has two chances.

If the card is a Jack, the player has one chance.

If the player cannot draw an Ace or face card within their allotted number of chances, their opponent adds the cards to their own pile. If the player can draw an Ace or face card, then the other player must draw for an Ace or face card of their own. Play continues until one player has all of the cards and wins the game.

GO FISH

Go Fish, or Authors, is a card game that requires two to five players and a standard deck of fifty-two playing cards. Go Fish is typically described as an easy game that young kids enjoy, but people of all ages can have fun playing it. The objective of Go Fish is to have the most "books," or four of a kinds, by the end of the game.

SETUP

Before gameplay can begin, a dealer must be selected. Each player draws one card from a shuffled deck. Aces are high and 2s are low. The player with the lowest card is the dealer. The dealer shuffles the cards. The player to the dealer's immediate right cuts the shuffled deck, and the dealer then passes the cards out face down, clockwise, and one at a time. If fewer than four people are playing, each player receives seven cards. If more than four people are playing, each player receives five cards. The remaining deck is placed face down in the middle of the circle to form the "ocean."

HOW TO PLAY

The game begins when the player to the left of the dealer "fishes" by asking another player if they have a certain card in their hand (e.g., "Do you have any Queens?"). If the player does have the type of card asked for, they must give the asker all of that type that they possess (e.g., if the player has three Queens, they must give the asker all three cards).

The asker can then continue questioning the same player, or they can move on to question a different player. They may also ask for another type of card, or they can ask for the same type of card they've requested previously. If a player does not have the type of card asked for, they say "Go fish," and the asker picks up the top card from the ocean. The gameplay then moves to the left and the next person fishes for cards.

A player makes a book when they have four of a kind. When a book is made, the player places the four cards face up in a pile in front of them to verify to the other players that they made a book. The game ends when all thirteen books are made. The player with the most books wins. If a player runs out of cards during the game, they may select one from the ocean when it is their turn. If there are no more cards in the ocean, they are out of the game and the number of books they have is final.

VARIATIONS

AUSTRALIAN GO FISH. For Australian Go Fish (which, as one might expect, is predominately played in Australia), books are made from two of a kinds instead of the traditional four of a kinds. With this variation, Jokers can also be used in gameplay.

MINUMAN. Minuman is an Indonesian version of Go Fish and means "drink" in English. For the most part, Minuman is similar to traditional Go Fish with the additional rule that players take a drink from an alcoholic beverage if they must draw from the ocean. When the game is finished, the loser must finish their entire drink if they have not already done so.

HAPPY FAMILIES. Happy Families is an old version of Go Fish invented by John Jaques Jr. in 1851. A Happy Families deck consists of forty-four illustrated cards. There are eleven families with four members each. The families are as follows: Block the Barber, Bones the Butcher, Bun the Baker, Bung the Brewer, Chip the Carpenter, Dip the Dyer, Dose the Doctor,

Grits the Grocer, Pots the Painter, Soot the Sweep, and Tape the Tailor. Every family member has a father, a mother, a son (master), and a daughter (miss). Like traditional Go Fish, cards are shuffled, dealt, and asked for to create a complete family. However, players must ask for specific family members.

BACKSTAB FISH. Backstab Fish is a variation of Go Fish that normally takes a lot longer than traditional Go Fish. Virtually all of the rules are the same, but two decks are in play with Jokers included. With 108 cards, Backstab Fish can be great in large groups, but it can also be enjoyed by a small number of patient players.

I DOUBT IT

I Doubt It is a classic party game (sometimes called BS or Bluff) suitable for three or more players of all ages. The game requires a standard deck of fifty-two playing cards. Kings are valued highest, and Aces are valued lowest. The objective of the game is to be the first person to get rid of all of their cards.

SETUP

Before gameplay can begin, a dealer must be selected. Players choose a random card from a shuffled deck. The player with the lowest card becomes the dealer. Ties are broken with repeated drawings. The dealer shuffles the deck and deals all of the cards face down, one at a time in a clockwise direction.

HOW TO PLAY

The game starts with Aces. The player to the immediate left of the dealer begins by stating how many Aces they will be putting face down in the middle of the gameplay area. Play moves clockwise, and the card rank for each turn increases incrementally as the game continues. So, once the first player lays down their Ace (or Aces), the next player must lay down 2s, and then the next player must lay down 3s, and so on.

Players have to lay down at least one card even if they do not have the specific card rank in their hand. For example, if the rank a player must lay down is a 5 and they have no 5s, they can secretly lay down a Queen and a Jack and say they are laying down two 5s.

Before the next player lays down their cards, anyone who thinks the current player is lying can say "I doubt it." The player who laid down their cards must turn the cards over and show them to the other players. If the player was lying, they must take all of the cards in the pile and add them to their hand. If the player was telling the truth, the player who said "I doubt it" must take all of the cards.

The first player to get rid of all of their cards wins the game.

NINETY-NINE

Ninety-Nine is a classic card game for two or more players. It requires a standard deck of fifty-two playing cards and is suitable for ages eight and up. The objective of Ninety-Nine is to avoid being the player who causes the value of the discard pile to increase above 99.

SETUP

Before gameplay can begin, a dealer must be selected. Every player draws a card from a shuffled deck. The player with the highest card becomes the first dealer. Ties are broken by a redraw. The dealer then shuffles the deck and deals three cards, face down and one at a time, to each player. The remaining deck forms the stock and is placed in the center of the table.

HOW TO PLAY

Starting with the player to the left of the dealer and going clockwise, players remove a card from their own hand and place it face up next to the stock to form the discard pile. The running value of the discard pile is recorded by all players. After adding a card to the discard pile, players replace it by drawing one card from the stock and adding it to their hand.

The game continues until someone is forced to play a card that brings the value of the discard pile above 99. If a player passes 99 three times, they are out of the game. The last player in the game is the winner.

SCORING

The following chart shows the card values in the game Ninety-Nine. Some cards have multiple values, and some cards allow players to pass or to reverse the flow of the game, so pay close attention:

Card Type	Value
2, 3	Points correspond to face value
4	Worth 0 points and allows a player to reverse the direction of play
5, 6, 7, 8	Points correspond to face value
9	Worth 0 points, and allows a player to pass on their turn
10	–10 points (negative 10)

Jack, Queen	10 points
King	Takes the count to exactly 99
Ace	1 or 11 (players must announce the value when the Ace is played)

VARIATIONS

Players can change up the card values in any way they choose in order to make the game more fun. The following is a list of alternative card values:

- Jokers are added to the deck and assigned a value of 10 points.
- The role of the 9 and King are swapped.
- 5s have a value of –5.
- Aces could be worth either 1 point or 14.
- Queens have a value of 0 and force the next player to play two cards.

OLD MAID

Old Maid is a card-matching game played with two or more people and a standard deck of fifty-two playing cards. This game is suitable for players of all ages, and the objective of the game is to pair up all of your cards and to avoid being the player holding the odd Queen, or "old maid," at the end of the game.

SETUP

Before the game begins, an initial dealer must be chosen. Every player is given a card from a shuffled deck, and whoever receives the highest card becomes the first dealer. Ties are broken by a repeated deal. For the dealer selection process, Aces are high and 2s are low.

Before dealing the cards, the dealer must first remove one Queen from the deck so that only fifty-one cards remain. The dealer then shuffles the remaining deck, and the player to their right cuts it. Finally, the dealer deals all of the cards one at a time in a clockwise direction. It is okay for some players to have more cards than others at the game's outset.

HOW TO PLAY

After everyone has received their cards, players remove any pairs they can from their hands and place them face down on the table in front of them.

Next, the dealer fans out the cards in their hand face down so that no one can see the cards and offers them to the player to their left. The player to the left of the dealer then chooses one random card from the dealer's hand and adds it to their own hand.

The player to the left of the dealer then tries to make another pair using this new card. If they succeed, the new pair is removed from their hand and added to their previously created pile of pairs. If they cannot create any new pairs, the card remains in their deck.

Then the player to the left of the dealer offers their hand face down to the player on their left and gameplay proceeds as before, with each player selecting a card and then creating pairs whenever possible.

Players can "go out" and be safe from becoming the old maid in one of two ways: They can pair up all of their cards, or the player to their left can take their last card as part of the drawing process that happens during each player's turn.

Because one of the Queens was removed, there will always be an unpaired Queen left at the end of each game. The player who is left holding this Queen becomes the old maid and loses.

HISTORY OF OLD MAID

The phrase *old maid* is an extremely rude way to refer to a childless and unmarried woman. The phrase was first coined in England as early as the eighteenth century, and the Old Maid card game began during the late Victorian period. Though its exact origins are unknown, one possible theory is that it derives from old English drinking games.

Historically, the old maid in the game has been represented as a negative figure; after all, the player who loses the game is the player who becomes the old maid. As early as the late 1800s, specialty Old Maid decks were created featuring unbecoming illustrations of the title figure. An 1890 deck, for example, includes a picture of an old woman wearing pants and riding a bike. While this might seem perfectly normal when judged by today's standards, it was considered to be highly insulting to Victorian sensibilities. Throughout the twentieth century, the image of the old maid on specialty decks shifted from the Victorian bike rider to the problematic stereotype of the "crazy old cat lady" and often showed older women knitting or sewing.

More recent players have done away with the Old Maid concept entirely, choosing instead to remove a different card from the deck. Anyone fancy a game of Old Jack?

PIG

Pig (also called Donkey) is a classic card game for four or more people of any age. It's played with a standard deck of fifty-two playing cards. In larger groups, two decks may be used. The objective of Pig is either to become the first player to achieve a four of a kind or to not be the last player to see that someone else has achieved a four of a kind.

SETUP

Before gameplay can begin, a dealer must be selected. Players choose a random card from a shuffled deck. The player with the lowest card becomes the dealer. Ties are broken with repeated drawings. The dealer shuffles the deck and then deals four cards, face down, to each player. The remaining stock is then placed to the right of the dealer.

HOW TO PLAY

The dealer begins the game by drawing a card from the stock. The dealer must then look at their own hand and the card they've just drawn and determine whether to keep the new card or pass it along to the next player. If the dealer keeps the new card, they must discard one of the four cards already in their hand to the player on their left. Players may only keep four cards in their hand at one time.

This pattern continues in a clockwise direction. Once a player receives a card, they then must discard a card by passing it to the player on their left. The goal is to form a four of a kind.

Once a player has gotten a four of a kind, they must place a finger on their nose. The other players must do the same as soon as they notice it. The last player to put a finger on their nose loses the round. Some people prefer to stick out their tongue instead of placing a finger on their nose—the choice is yours.

VARIATION

SPOONS. In Spoons, instead of placing a finger on their nose, players grab a spoon from the center of the group once a player has gotten a four of a kind. There is always one fewer spoon than the number of players, so the person who does not get a spoon loses the round.

SIX-CARD GOLF

Six-Card Golf is a game for two to four players that uses a standard deck of fifty-two playing cards with two Jokers added. The objective of Six-Card Golf is to have the lowest number of points after nine rounds or "holes." This game is best suited for players ages eight and up.

SETUP

Before gameplay can begin, a dealer must be selected. Each player draws one card from a shuffled deck. The player with the lowest card becomes the dealer. The dealer shuffles the deck and deals six cards face down to each player, moving in a clockwise direction. The remaining cards are then placed in the center of the table to form the stock. The top card from the stock is then placed face up next to the stock to create the discard pile.

Without looking at their hand, players arrange their cards in a three-by-two grid, making sure to keep all of their cards facing down, like so:

HOW TO PLAY

Play begins with the player to the left of the dealer and proceeds clockwise. On their first turn, and only on their first turn, players must flip over two of their six cards. Once a player has turned over two cards, they must then decide to either draw from the stock in the middle of the table or from the discard pile.

If the player does not want to keep the card they've drawn, they simply place the card on the discard pile. If they want to keep the card they've drawn, players must switch out any cards in their grid for the new card. If the new card replaces a face-down card, it should be turned face up when it is laid down. Finally, the player must then discard so that they only have six cards total left in their grid.

After the first round, players continue moving in a clockwise direction, with each player drawing a new card from either the discard pile or the stock. Each time a player replaces a card in their hand that's currently facing down, the new card must be placed face up so it can be seen by the other players.

Once a player turns all of their cards face up, they are out and every other player has one more turn to draw a new card. After the round has ended, all cards that are still face down must be flipped over.

If the game is still going and the stock runs out, the discard pile is shuffled to form a new stock. The top card of the stock is flipped over to form the new discard pile.

SCORING

Points are tallied based on the value of the cards and their arrangement in the columns. The player with the lowest score at the end of nine rounds wins.

Card Type	Value
Ace	1 point
2–10	Points correspond to face value
Jack, Queen	10 points
King	0 points
Joker	–2 points

If two cards in the same column form a pair (say two Aces or two 7s), the point total for that column is 0.

SLAPJACK

Slapjack, or Slaps, is a game for two to four players. It is played with a standard deck of fifty-two playing cards. The objective of Slapjack is to win all of the cards by quickly slapping the deck whenever a Jack is played. This game is suitable for players of all ages.

SETUP

Before gameplay can begin, a dealer must be selected. Each player draws one card from a shuffled deck. The player with the lowest card becomes the dealer. The dealer shuffles the deck and deals all of the cards one at a time and face down, moving in a clockwise direction. Players may not look at the cards they have been dealt. It is okay for some players to have more cards than others at the game's outset.

HOW TO PLAY

Starting with the person to the left of the dealer and going clockwise, players place the top card of their deck in the center of the table. Players must draw cards away from themselves and toward the center of the table so that all players can see the card's value at the same time. If the card drawn is a Jack, players try to be the first one to slap the pile. Whichever player slaps first wins all of the cards in the pile. The pile is then shuffled and added to the winner's hand so that no one knows where the Jack is placed. The winner of that pile then draws the top card from their hand to restart play.

If players slap the pile when no Jack is present, that player must give a card to the player who laid down the previous card.

When a person runs out of cards, they have one chance to win a slap. If a player runs out of cards, a Jack is played on the next player's turn, and they lose the slap, that player is out of the game.

If a card is played on top of a Jack before anyone can slap it, the Jack is lost and play continues.

The player who eventually gets all of the cards wins.

SNAP

Snap is a popular children's card game that requires quick-wittedness and agility. The game uses a standard deck of fifty-two playing cards and is meant for two to eight players. The objective of Snap is to win all of the cards in the deck.

SETUP

Before gameplay can begin, a dealer must be selected. Players choose a random card from a shuffled deck. The player with the lowest card becomes the dealer. Ties are broken with repeated drawings. The dealer shuffles the deck and deals all of the cards face down, one at a time in a clockwise direction. Players should not look at their cards. It is okay for some players to have more cards than others at the game's outset.

HOW TO PLAY

Gameplay begins, starting with the player to the left of the dealer and proceeding clockwise. On their turn, each player flips up the top card in their pile and places it toward the center of the table, building a discard pile. Each player should have their own personal discard pile, and should not combine their discarded playing cards with any of their opponents' discards.

Players must draw cards away from themselves and toward the center of the table so that all players can see the card's value at the same time.

If two cards in different discard piles form a pair (e.g., a 6 of hearts and a 6 of spades), any player may shout "Snap!" and receive the cards in both piles. If two or more players shout "Snap!" at the same time and it can't be judged who said it first, the cards go to the middle of the table and form the Snap pot. If the top card from the Snap pot pairs with any of the players' top cards going forward, someone may shout "Snap pot!" and receive all of the cards in the Snap pot in addition to the player's pile. The player who wins all of the cards wins the game.

If a player flips up all of their cards, the flipped-up pile is shuffled to form a new pile.

When a player runs out of cards, they have one chance to win cards during the next Snap occurrence. If the player does not say "Snap" at the first opportunity, or if an opponent says it before them, that player is out of the game.

SNIP, SNAP, SNOREM

Snip, Snap, Snorem is a classic card-shedding game for three or more players. The game requires a standard deck of fifty-two playing cards. Kings are high, and Aces are low. The objective of Snip, Snap, Snorem is to be the first to lose all of your cards. This game is suitable for players ages eight and up.

SETUP

Before gameplay can begin, a dealer must be selected. To do so, players choose a random card from a shuffled deck. The player with the lowest card becomes the dealer. Ties are broken with repeated drawings. The dealer shuffles the deck and deals all of the cards face down, one at a time, to every player, moving clockwise. It is okay if some players have more cards than others at the game's outset.

HOW TO PLAY

The player to the left of the dealer begins gameplay by looking at their hand and placing any card or cards from their hand in the middle of the game area. Going clockwise, players try to complete the set. For example, if the first person played a 7 of clubs, the next player would try to play a 7 of spades, diamonds, or hearts.

Players should discard all of the cards of the same rank that they have in their respective hands. For instance, if a player has a 7 of spades and a 7 of diamonds, they should play both cards at the same time.

If a player cannot build on the set, their turn is passed to the player on their left.

Players must say "Snip," "Snap," or "Snorem" when building on a set. Whoever plays the second card in the set must say "Snip." Whoever plays the third card has to say "Snap" and whoever plays the fourth card says "Snorem."

Continuing with the example provided above: If the first player lays down a 7 of clubs, they simply say "Seven." If the player to their left lays down both the 7 of spades and the 7 of diamonds, they must say "Snip" after they lay down the 7 of spades and "Snap" after they lay down the 7 of diamonds.

The player who lays down the fourth card in the set must then say "Snorem." This player is also responsible for beginning the next set by playing a card or cards from their own hand.

The first player to run out of cards wins the game.

SOLITAIRE

Solitaire, Klondike, or Patience (as it is called in Europe) is a game for one player and uses a standard deck of fifty-two playing cards. The objective of Solitaire is to organize a shuffled deck of cards into four stacks (one for each suit) in ascending order (Ace to King).

SETUP

In Solitaire, there are four types of piles: the tableau, the stock, the talon, and the foundations.

THE TABLEAU. The tableau consist of seven piles and is where most of the gameplay occurs. The first pile has one card, the second pile has two cards, and so on until there are seven piles, with the last having seven cards. Only the top card in each pile is turned face up.

THE STOCK. The remaining cards after building the tableau are referred to as the stock.

THE TALON. The talon is a pile of three cards that is drawn from the stock. Only the top card of the talon may be played.

THE FOUNDATIONS. The foundations consist of four stacks of cards (one for each suit) that are arranged in ascending order (Ace to King). At the beginning of the game, the foundation piles will be empty.

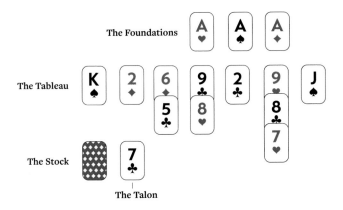

HOW TO PLAY

Within the tableau, face-up cards are arranged in descending order (King to Ace) and by alternating color. For example, a black 8 may be moved onto a red 9, and a red Queen may be moved onto a black King. A card may be stacked on top of another card only if the bottom card is a different color and one number higher. The player may transfer the top card or an entire stack of face-up cards to any of the tableau piles in an attempt to create a new sequence of descending value and alternating color.

An empty spot in the tableau may only be filled with a King. If the player cannot move any cards within the tableau, three cards are drawn from the top of the stock to form the talon.

If the top card in the talon cannot be played, three more cards are selected from the stock. If the stock runs out, the talon pile is reshuffled to form a new stock and the process continues. For easier games, the talon may be reduced from three cards to one card.

While a player is moving cards within the tableau, they should also be trying to build up the foundations from Ace to King. Only the top card from the talon or the tableau piles may be transferred to the foundations. The top card on any foundation pile may be moved back to the tableau if needed.

When all cards have been transferred to the foundations in ascending order (Ace to King), the game is won.

If no more moves can be made and the foundatios piles are incomplete, the game is lost.

VARIATIONS

There are far too many variations of Solitaire to list them all. Here are a few of the most popular versions:

BOWLING SOLITAIRE. Bowling Solitaire requires a deck with no face cards, Aces through 10s only. Aces have a value of 1, and the other cards are valued by their number. The player shuffles the deck and sets up the "pins" by building a four-row pyramid of face-up cards; the first row has one card, the second row has two cards, and so on. The player then sets up the "bowling balls" by making three piles. The first pile has five cards, the second has three cards, and the third has two cards. Only the top card is flipped up in each bowling ball pile.

The player then uses the bowling ball piles to try to knock down pins. A player can knock down pins in three ways:

1.   The pin card and the ball card have the same value.
2.   Two or more pin cards equal the value of the ball card.
3.   The last digit of the pin cards equals the value of the ball card. For example, the ball card is a 6, and there are two pin cards equaling 16, such as two 8s.

Like regular bowling, the player has two bowls per set of pins before they reshuffle the pin cards and make a new pyramid. If they cannot knock down any pins, it is a gutter ball and they move on to the next ball pile. Scoring is done like regular bowling.

EMPEROR. Emperor is one of the most time-consuming Solitaire games out there and is very similar to Spider (described below). Emperor is played with two standard decks of fifty-two playing cards. Ten piles are dealt consisting of four cards each. The first three cards in each pile are placed face down while the fourth card in each pile is placed face up.

Cards cannot be moved in groups; they must be moved one at a time. The goal is to release the Aces and build up the eight foundations out of the tableau.

FORTY THIEVES. Forty Thieves (sometimes called Napoleon at St. Helena) is similar to basic Solitaire, but it doubles the number of cards. There are ten tableau piles with initially four cards in each pile (making up the forty thieves). The tableau is built upon a descending sequence (King to Ace) of the same suit, instead of alternating color. Any card may fill an empty space. There are eight foundations, and, like basic Solitaire, the game is won when all cards are transferred to the foundations in ascending order and in separated suits.

SPIDER. Spider is a much more difficult version of traditional Solitaire. In Spider, there are two decks of cards in play, ten tableau piles, no foundation piles, and no talon pile. The objective in Spider is to sequence thirteen cards of the same suit in descending order (King to Ace) within a tableau pile. When thirteen cards are sequenced, the cards are removed. If no moves can be made within the tableau piles, one card from the stock is given to each tableau pile. You cannot play on a tableau pile that is in an out-of-order sequence. The game is won when there are no more cards.

YUKON. Yukon is a Solitaire game that uses a standard deck of fifty-two playing cards. In Yukon, there are no stock or talon piles. All fifty-two cards are used to make up a seven-pile tableau at the start of the game. To set up a Yukon game, the player first makes a traditional seven-pile tableau with all cards facing down. Then piles two through seven receive an additional five cards, all face up. The objective of the tableau and the foundations is similar to traditional Solitaire with the additional rule that any group of face-up cards may be moved within the tableau regardless of sequence.

HISTORY OF SOLITAIRE

Solitaire is a puzzle game that boasts a wonderful history. Originating in Germany, the game was first recorded in the royal game book *Das Neue Königliche L'Hombre-Spiel* in 1788. Some early evidence suggests that Solitaire began as a fortune-telling game and only later became a game of strategy. Some variants of Solitaire are still used for cartomancy (fortune-telling using a deck of cards) today. From the Rhineland, the Solitaire craze moved west into France. From the French, we get many of the terms still used in Solitaire. For example, *tableau* is *table* in French and *talon* is *heel*. A popular rumor is that while Napoleon was exiled, he spent most of his days playing Solitaire. Solitaire became increasingly popular throughout the nineteenth century and continued moving westward into England, with Queen Victoria's German husband, Prince Albert, being a notable lover of the game. In 1874, the first collection of Solitaire games in the English language were published in *Illustrated Games of Patience* by Lady Adelaide Cadogan. Solitaire's popularity steadily increased throughout the twentieth century and became widely accessible in the 1980s, when computer engineers developed a free digital version of the game.

SPIT

Spit is a classic game played with two players and a standard deck of fifty-two playing cards. The objective of the game is to get rid of all of your cards. This game is appropriate for all ages, but speed is paramount, and the game works best when opponents are well matched.

SETUP

Before gameplay can begin, a dealer must be selected. Each player draws one card from a shuffled deck. The player with the lowest card becomes the dealer. The dealer shuffles the deck and deals all of the cards face down, one at a time, until each player has twenty-six cards. Players do not look at their cards.

Players then build up five stacks to form a tableau, which is a basic gameplay layout that looks similar to Solitaire. The first stack contains one card, the second stack contains two cards, and so on, until five stacks are made. The top card of each stack should be turned face up, while the other cards remain face down.

Each player should be left with eleven cards in their hands. These cards are referred to collectively as the spit pile. Players keep their spit pile in their hands, but may not look at any of the cards in their spit pile.

HOW TO PLAY

To begin, each player flips over the top card of their spit pile and places it toward the center of the table, separate from the other player's card. Players then begin to move cards around in order to get rid of all the cards in their tableau.

Cards may be moved in three different ways. First, each top card in a player's tableau may be moved onto either of the center cards if the rank of the card is one higher or one lower than the card in the center. Once a top card is moved into the center, the player should flip over the card below and continue to work their way through their tableau piles.

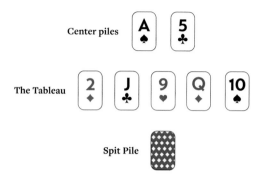

Center piles

The Tableau

Spit Pile

Second, players may also move cards within their own tableau piles as long as the cards match (as in Solitaire). In Spit, Aces can be both high and low, which means they can be played on both a King and a 2.

Third, cards of matching ranks may be stacked on top of each other within a player's tableau piles.

Once a pile is emptied of all its cards, players may move any card from another pile to fill the empty space. Players may not have more than five piles at any time, but they can have fewer as play continues.

There are no turns in Spit. Instead, players try to get rid of their tableau as soon as possible. If no player can play any cards into the two center piles, each player must then flip over the top card in their spit pile and add it to the center piles in order to restart play.

As soon as one player gets rid of their tableau, both players must quickly slap one of the two center piles. The first player to do so keeps the pile they slap, while the other player gets the other pile. Because the objective of this game is to ultimately get rid of all of your cards, players should try to slap the pile with the fewest cards. After each round, players will shuffle their cards and build a new tableau. Play continues until one player runs out of cards.

If both players are stuck and neither player has a spit pile left, the round is over and players try to slap the pile with the fewest cards.

When a player has fifteen or fewer cards, they must build their five-pile tableau until their cards run out. They will not have a spit pile and there will only be one center pile for both players to play off of.

WAR

War, or Battle, is typically played with two players of any age, although more players may be added. A standard deck of fifty-two playing cards is used. In War, cards are ranked Aces high and 2s low. The objective of the game is to win all of the cards in the deck.

SETUP

Before gameplay can begin, a dealer must be selected. Each player draws one card from a shuffled deck. The player with the lowest card becomes the dealer. The dealer shuffles the deck and deals all of the cards, face down and one at a time. Players do not look at their cards.

HOW TO PLAY

Both players place the top card of their stack onto the center of the table. The player whose card is higher in value takes both cards and places them in a separate pile next to their stack. Once a player runs out of cards in their stack, they shuffle all of the cards in their win pile and continue to play.

If each player lays down a card of the same value, then there is a "war." Players must then place three of their cards face down on the table and draw a fourth card from their stack, which is placed face up on the table. Whichever player lays down the card of the highest value takes all ten cards. If both cards in the second draw are also equal, the process is repeated and three more cards are laid face down, with a fourth card laid face up to determine a winner.

The player who wins all of the cards wins the game.

PLAYING CARDS AS
WEAPONS OF WAR

We all know that playing card games can become very competitive. The American humorist Finley Peter Dunne once said, "There are no friends at cards or world politics." Similarly, the British essayist Charles Lamb once wrote, "Cards are war, in disguise of a sport."

But how about using playing cards as an actual weapon of war? You could injure someone seriously if you learned to throw playing cards like card-throwing world record holder Rick Smith Jr., who can throw a playing card accurately and quickly enough to slice a piece of fruit in half. But playing cards have also been used in subtler ways during actual, real-life battles. Here are a few fascinating examples.

THE BATTLE OF SAN JACINTO

When General Sam Houston led Texas to freedom in 1836 in the battle of San Jacinto—the decisive battle of the Texas Revolution and part of the war for independence from Mexico—there were Mexicans fighting on both sides. So how could the Tejanos, who were Mexicans fighting for freedom as part of the Texan army, be distinguished from the Mexican army fighting to maintain control of the land?

Here's the solution General Houston apparently came up with: He instructed the Tejanos to put playing cards in their hat bands so that the Texans could easily differentiate between them and the Mexican soldiers. Doesn't that give a whole new meaning to *showing your hand*?

WORLD WAR II

In World War II, playing card manufacturer USPCC teamed up with military forces to create decks of cards that had an escape map printed between the two thin paper panels that are stuck together to make each card. Each card hid one segment of the overall map. After the cards were soaked in water and the two layers were peeled apart to access the secret map segments, these pieces could be puzzled together to create a complete

map, Allied prisoners could use it to help them escape from German POW camps and get out of Nazi Germany. The decks were delivered to POWs as part of seemingly innocuous Red Cross packages.

You can still buy an escape map deck today, though fortunately the map featured on this commemorative deck is printed on the card faces, so you don't need to ruin the deck in order to make the map.

VIETNAM WAR

In the Vietnam War, decks that consisted solely of the Ace of spades were produced for American soldiers. It was believed that this card was considered a symbol of death by the Vietnamese opposition forces, so American soldiers would wear the cards on their helmets as a sort of harbinger of doom. The idea was that members of the Viet Cong were superstitious, and seeing this Ace of spades would terrify them.

In retrospect, this practice appears to have been based on a false belief about the Viet Cong. But regardless of whether or not this psychological warfare actually worked on the enemy, it certainly did help improve morale of American troops, who believed they had a little piece of luck on their side.

INVASION OF IRAQ

Troops that were part of the 2003 invasion of Iraq were issued playing cards that featured pictures and information about the fifty-two most wanted members of Saddam Hussein's government, with Saddam himself featured on the Ace of spades. Members of the armed forces would often play cards during their downtime, and this "most wanted" deck helped them to become familiar with the names, faces, and titles of wanted Iraqis so they could more easily recognize them in the field.

This was not the first time that playing cards have been used in this fashion, with previous instances occurring in the US Civil War, World War II, and the Korean War. There have also been reports of US soldiers handing out playing cards as calling cards during Operation Iraqi Freedom and during Operation Enduring Freedom in Afghanistan; these cards would include an anonymous tip line phone number that locals could use.

ORDNANCE RECOGNITION

Multiple decks of playing cards are designed with an educational purpose: illustrating unexploded ammunition and weapons that the public might stumble upon by accident in war zones. These decks are aimed at assisting people at risk (e.g., soldiers, civilians, aid workers, de-miners) and helping them to identify and learn about the threats they face from unexploded ordnance.

Such ordnance recognition decks are still in use today. They are typically purchased by UN and government agencies to distribute to their staff and local citizens, and it is believed that these decks have helped save many lives and limbs.

AIRPLANE AND NAVAL SPOTTERS

Airplane spotter decks have also been used in times of war to assist antiaircraft gunners in recognizing enemy aircraft silhouettes, thereby ensuring that gunners fired only at the enemy and not at any of the allied forces. The cards identify fifty-two different aircraft, including Allied bombers and fighters, as well as Axis aircraft from Germany, Japan, and Italy. Each card features detailed silhouettes shown from three different angles:

front view, side view, and a view of the bottom of the aircraft, as it would have been seen by a ground observer. Naval spotter decks were also produced, and these decks featured cards with silhouettes of US and foreign warships from the 1940s to the 1960s.

These decks served a dual purpose as a source of entertainment and as a teaching aid. Soldiers would often play cards during downtime, and using the card faces as a way of making them familiar with important information was a genius idea. Replicas of these spotter decks are still available today from US Games Systems.

COLD CASES

Playing cards have also been used to help generate leads in unsolved murder cases. Details from unsolved crimes and victim photos have been printed on the faces of cards, and these decks have been given to prison inmates in lockup across the United States.

At least forty cold cases have been solved as a direct result of tips that were provided based on these cold case card decks. Who would have ever thought that a prison poker game could have this kind of payoff?

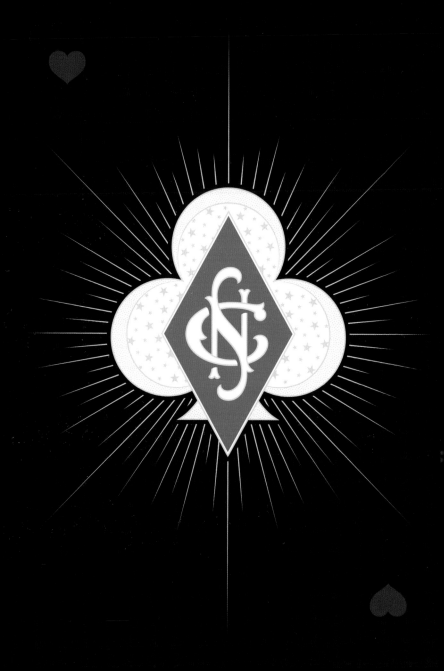

RUMMY GAMES

Rummy games are a group of games that revolve around the simple concept of matching cards of the same rank or sequences of the same suit. These beloved games have multiple variations and are played in all corners of the world.

RUMMY

Rummy or Rum is a traditional card-matching game that requires two to six players and a standard deck of fifty-two playing cards. Kings are high, and Aces are low. The objective of Rummy is to have the most points at the end of the game. A player earns points by forming sets, or melds, which consist of groups of three or four of a kind, or runs consisting of three or four cards of the same suit.

SETUP

Before gameplay can begin, a dealer must be selected. Each player draws one card from a shuffled deck. The player who draws the lowest card becomes the dealer. The dealer shuffles the deck and deals cards one at a time in a clockwise direction, starting with the player sitting to the dealer's left. If two people play, each player receives ten cards. If three or four people are playing, each person receives seven cards. If you have five or six players, each person receives six cards. The remaining cards are placed face down in a neat stack in the center of the table. These cards form the stock. The top card of the stock is flipped face up and placed next to the stack, forming the discard pile.

HOW TO PLAY

Play begins with the player sitting to the left of the dealer. At the beginning of each player's turn, a player must select one card from either the stock or the discard pile. If at any point in the game the stock runs out, the discard pile is shuffled to form a new stock, and the top card in the new stock becomes the first card in the discard pile. The general goal of the game is to get rid of your cards as quickly as possible, thereby earning points. This can be done in three ways: melding, laying off, or discarding.

MELDING. A player makes a meld by having either three or more of a kind or three or more of a run.

A meld of three or more of a kind is made when a player obtains three or more cards of the same numerical value, like so:

A run is made of three or more cards of the same suit in increasing or decreasing order.

When a player makes a meld, they must lay it face up on the table. Melding is optional, and a player can play only one meld per turn; they may not play all of their melds at once.

LAYING OFF. A player may also get rid of cards by building upon melds created by other players. For instance, if one player has made a meld of three Kings and the player whose turn it is has the fourth King, they may place it on the three-King meld to complete the set. Likewise, if a meld is made of the 2, 3, and 4 of clubs and the player in play has the Ace of clubs, they may place it before the 2 to build upon the run. Laying off is optional, and there is no limit to the number of cards a player can lay off, though they must wait until it is their turn to lay off any cards. A player can lay off in the same turn that they meld.

DISCARDING. At the end of every turn, a player must choose one card to add to the discard pile. If the player drew a card from the discard pile to begin their turn, they may not discard that same card to end their turn.

SCORING

When one player gets rid of all of their cards, all other players must stop and tally up their points based on the remaining cards in their hand. Points are given by card value, with Aces counting as 1 point and face cards counting as 10 points. The tallied points are then awarded to the player who got rid of their cards first.

Card Type	Value
Ace	1 point
2, 3, 4, 5, 6, 7, 8, 9	points correspond to value
10, J, Q, K	10 points

DECLARING RUMMY

A player can declare Rummy if they are able to get rid of all of their cards in only one move. This can be done by opting out of making moves and strategically waiting for the right runs and melds to appear on the table. A player may not declare Rummy if they have already played any of their cards. If a player is able to declare Rummy, the points tallied from the other players are doubled.

GAMEPLAY EXAMPLE

Suppose you are playing a four-person game of Rummy. The deck has been dealt, there's a King of hearts in the discard pile, and you hold the King of spades; the 5, 6, and 7 of diamonds; and the 2, 8, and Jack of hearts.

The player to your right places a meld of three 2s on the table and then discards a 3 of hearts. It is now your turn. You begin by selecting a card from the stock and get the King of diamonds.

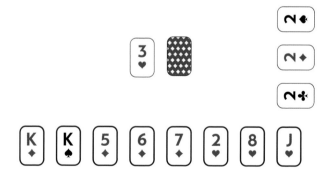

You place the run of diamonds on the table and lay off the 2 of hearts on the meld of 2s. You then discard the Jack of hearts. After your turn is completed, you have the King of spades, the King of diamonds, and the 8 of hearts left in your hand.

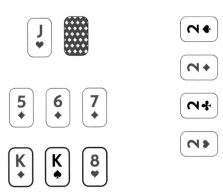

A round passes and a meld of 8s has been placed by the player on your left, who then discards a 4 of spades.

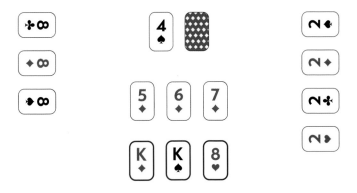

At the start of your turn, you select from the stock and receive the King of clubs.

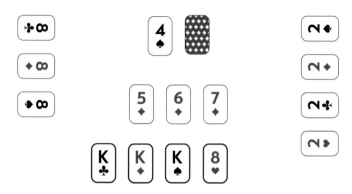

You place the meld of Kings on the table and discard the 8 of hearts, making you win the game.

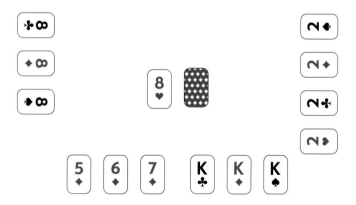

You could also play your 8 of hearts on the meld of 8s laid down by the player on your left. You can go out by melding, laying off, or discarding your last card. The choice is yours.

GIN RUMMY

Gin Rummy, which is also referred to simply as Gin, is a traditional card-matching game that requires two players. It uses a standard deck of fifty-two playing cards. Kings are high, and Aces are low. In Gin Rummy, cards are worth their numerical value with Aces worth 1 and face cards worth 10. The objective of Gin Rummy is to be the first player to reach 100 points.

SETUP

Before gameplay can begin, a dealer must be selected. Each player draws one card from a shuffled deck. The player who draws the lowest card becomes the dealer. The dealer then shuffles the deck and deals ten cards to each player one at a time. The remaining cards are placed face down in the center of the group to form the stock. The top card of the stock is then flipped face up and placed next to the stock to form the discard pile.

HOW TO PLAY

The non-dealer has the option to play first by taking the top card from the discard pile. If they choose to pass, the dealer then has the choice to take the top card from the discard pile. If the dealer also chooses to pass, the other player then begins the game by drawing the top card from the stock. From the first draw onward, each player must pick up a card from either the stock or the discard pile to begin their turn; each player must also remove one card from their hand and place it in the discard pile to end their turn.

The general goal is to get rid of deadwood by melding as many cards as you can in order to "go knock" or "go gin." Deadwood refers to any cards that cannot be used to form a meld. If neither player can reach knock or gin by the time the stock has only two cards left, no points are awarded, and the hand is finished.

MELDING. Just as in traditional Rummy, a player makes a meld by either having three or more of a kind, or by having three or more of a run. A run is made of three or more cards of the same suit in either increasing or decreasing order. Unlike in traditional Rummy, players do not lay down their melds in Gin Rummy until someone goes knock.

KNOCKING AND LAYING OFF. A player can go knock when the card value of their deadwood is 10 or less. To go knock, a player must first place whichever card they plan to discard face down on the discard pile. The player who is knocking places all of their cards face up on the table. The non-knocking player now has the opportunity to lay off their deadwood cards onto the knocking player's melds. For instance, if the knocking player has made a meld of three Kings and their opponent has the fourth King, they may place it on the three-King meld to complete the set and reduce their deadwood. Likewise, if a meld is made of the 2, 3, and 4 of clubs and the player in play has the Ace of clubs, they may place it before the 2 to build upon the run.

UNDERCUTTING. If the non-knocking player has fewer points for their deadwood than the knocking player, it is known as an undercut and the non-knocking player receives the points along with a 10-point bonus.

GOING GIN. A player goes gin if they get rid of all of their cards through melds. Going gin results in a 25-point bonus along with the deadwood value tabulated from the other player's hand.

SCORING

Once no more cards can be played, both players tabulate their deadwood according to the same scoring rules as basic Rummy, with Aces low and Kings high.

If the match ended in a knock and there was no undercut, points are given to the knocking player based on the difference between the card values of the remaining deadwood in the game. Here's a quick reference to the cards and their assigned point values, using the club suit as an example:

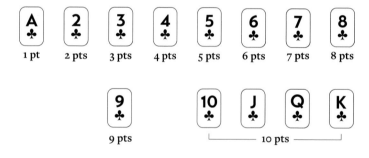

GAMEPLAY EXAMPLE

The deck has been dealt and you have the following hand: the Ace, 4, 6, 7, Jack, and King of spades; the Ace of diamonds; and the 5, 9, and Queen of clubs. The card in the discard pile is the Queen of spades.

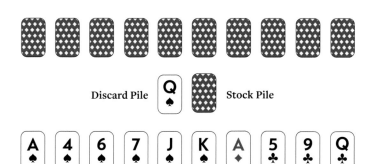

Discard Pile

Stock Pile

On your turn, you select the Queen of spades from the discard pile and discard your initial Queen of clubs to form a run of spades (Jack, Queen, and King).

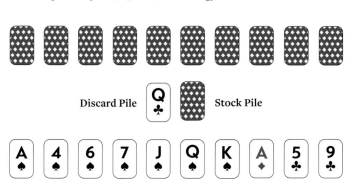

Discard Pile

Stock Pile

The other player takes their turn. You draw from the stock and receive the 2 of diamonds and discard the 9 of clubs.

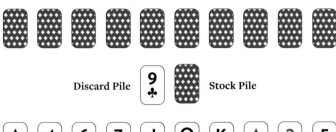

On your next turn you draw the 8 of spades and discard the 5 of clubs. Your hand is now two melds (a run of the Jack, Queen, and King of spades, and a run of the 6, 7, and 8 of spades) and four deadwood cards (an Ace and 4 of spades and the Ace and 2 of diamonds).

The other player knocks with the 9 of hearts as their only deadwood. Because your deadwood cards are valued at 8,

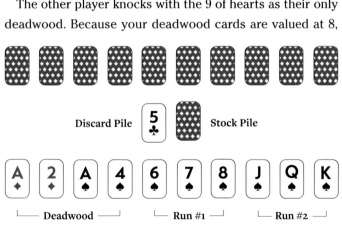

you undercut their knock and win the round. The 10-point undercut bonus plus the difference of deadwood cards (9–8) gives you a total of 11 points for the round.

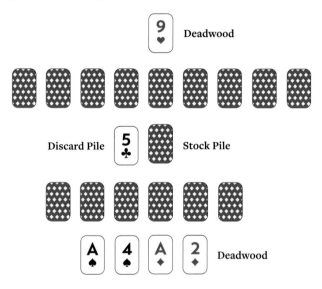

CANASTA

Canasta is a Rummy-type game of melding that is played with two standard decks of fifty-two playing cards plus four Jokers. The game is traditionally played with four players, who are split up into teams of two. The objective of Canasta is to be the first team to reach 5,000 points.

SETUP

Before the game begins, an initial dealer must be chosen. To do so, every player is given a card from a shuffled deck, and whoever receives the highest card becomes the first dealer. If two players draw the same high card, a tie is broken by a repeated deal. The initial dealer shuffles the deck and then offers the deck to the player on their right, who cuts the deck. The dealer deals eleven cards one at a time to each of the four players, starting on their left and moving clockwise. The remaining cards are placed face down in the center of the table, and this becomes the stock. The top card of the stock is turned face up and placed to the side to form the discard pile. The dealer position rotates clockwise at the end of each round.

Teammates must sit across from each other and work together to form more melds than their opponents.

HOW TO PLAY

Gameplay moves clockwise and starts with the player on the dealer's left. At the beginning of their turn, each player must draw a card from either the stock or the discard pile. A player is always entitled to draw a card from the stock, but in order to take a card from the discard pile, the player must take all of the cards in the pile. In addition, the top card in the pile must either combine with another card in the player's hand to begin a meld or build upon one that has already been made. Once the player has drawn a card, they may then lay down a meld (optional) before discarding. If a player finds a red 3 in their hand, that player must place the red 3 face up on the table during their next turn and draw a replacement card from the stock. If a player finds a red 3 when they take the discard pile, the player must place the red 3 face up on the table but does not draw a replacement card.

Players continue to build upon melds in hopes of getting a canasta, which is a meld of seven or more cards. Team members may choose to lay down melds in front of one or both players. Once a team has at least one canasta, and at least one of the players on the team has run out of cards, the team can then go out and end the round.

MELDING. Melds are formed by matching at least three cards of the same rank. Unlike other games inspired by Rummy, a meld cannot be created by forming a run of three or more cards. In order to be awarded points for a meld, the meld must be placed face up on the card table.

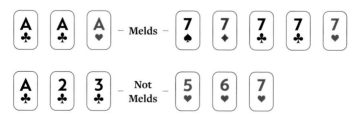

WILD CARDS. The four Jokers and eight 2s in the deck are wild cards and can be used to build upon any meld. However, melds must be composed of more natural cards than wild cards, and Jokers and 2s may not be used to make melds on their own, without natural cards.

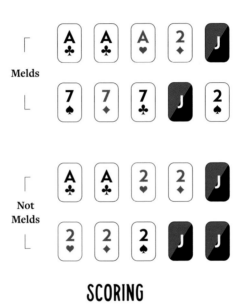

SCORING

In Canasta, points are awarded in four different ways: card values, canastas, red 3s, and going out.

CARD VALUES. In Canasta, Jokers are worth 50 points, Aces and 2s are worth 20 points, Kings through 8s are worth 10 points, and 4s through 7s and black 3s are worth 5 points. The value of unmelded cards is subtracted from the value of melded cards.

CANASTAS. A meld composed of seven or more cards is referred to as a canasta. A canasta that is formed without any wild cards is worth 500 points. A canasta that includes wild cards is worth 300 points.

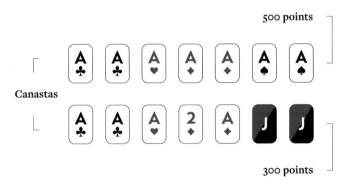

RED 3. Each red 3 in the deck is worth 100 points on its own. However, if one team manages to collect all four of the red 3s, they receive 800 points.

100 points   └── 800 points ──┘

GOING OUT. Once a team has formed at least one canasta and one member of the team has run out of cards, the team can then go out. The first team to do this receives an additional 100 points.

ADDITIONAL RULES

The first meld a player makes must have a minimum meld value that depends on the team's current score. For a team score of 0–1,499, the first meld a player makes must be at least 50 points. For a team score of 1,500–2,999, the first meld a player makes must be at least 90 points. For a team score of 3,000+, the first meld a player makes must be at least 120 points.

The discard pile becomes frozen (i.e., nobody can take from it) when a player decides to discard a wild card. The discard pile can become unfrozen if a player can make a natural meld by using the top card in the discard pile.

VARIATIONS

TWO-PLAYER CANASTA. In Two-Player Canasta, fifteen cards are initially dealt. If a player draws from the stock, they must draw two cards instead of the usual one. Additionally, a player needs to complete two canastas in order to go out and end the round. All other rules of Canasta apply, including the 5,000-point objective.

SAMBA. Samba is basically Canasta but with increased values for everything. Three standard decks of fifty-two playing cards plus Jokers are in play, totaling 162 cards. Instead of a 5,000-point objective, teams have to reach 10,000 points. Melds can be made by cards of a kind and cards in sequence. Six red 3s are worth 1,000 points. Melds can only have two wild cards in them. For teams with 7,000 points or more, the first meld a player makes must be at least 150 points.

SCORING VARIATIONS

Many scoring variations can be applied to Canasta, based on skill level and time commitment. Some common variations include:

- A natural canasta of 7s is worth 2,500.
- A canasta of wild cards is worth 2,000.
- A mixed canasta of 7s is a penalty of 2,500.
- If players have three or more Aces in their hand at the end of the round, there is a penalty of 1,500.

HAND AND FOOT

Hand and Foot is a popular card game for four or six players derived from Rummy and Canasta. It can be described as a simpler, easier version of Canasta that is often played by beginners. Hand and Foot uses either five (for four players) or six (for six players) standard decks of fifty-two playing cards plus four Jokers. The objective of Hand and Foot is to be the first to get rid of all of your cards and for your team to have the most points.

SETUP

Before the game begins, an initial dealer must be chosen. Every player is given a card from a shuffled deck, and whoever receives the highest card becomes the first dealer. Ties are broken by a repeated deal. The initial dealer shuffles the deck and the player to their right cuts it. The dealer then deals two sets of eleven cards, one at a time and clockwise, to each of the four players. The first set of eleven is called the hand, and the last set of eleven is called the foot. The remaining cards are placed face down to form the stock. The top card of the stock is turned face up and placed to the side to form the discard pile. The dealer position rotates clockwise at the end of each round.

Teammates sit across from each other and work together to form more melds than the other team(s).

HOW TO PLAY

The gameplay moves clockwise and begins with the player located to the left of the dealer. At the beginning of their turn, they must take a card from either the stock or the discard pile. To take a card from the discard pile, the top card must either combine with another card in the player's hand to begin a meld or build upon one already made. If a player takes from the discard pile, they must take all of the cards in the discard pile. To end a turn, the player must discard one card.

Players must start playing with their hand pile while their foot pile is laid face down. Once a player has played all of the cards in their hand pile, they may then pick up their foot pile.

MELDING. Melds are formed by matching cards of the same rank. A meld must begin with at least three cards. Melds are shared within the teams, so teammates can build upon each other's melds. As in Canasta, a run of three cards in sequential order is not considered a meld.

WILD CARDS. The Jokers and 2s in the deck are wild cards and can be used to build upon any meld. However, melds must have more natural cards than wild cards.

BOOKS. In Hand and Foot, a meld of seven cards is called a book. If none of those cards are wild, it is called a red book. If any of the cards are wild, it is called a black book. When books are made, the pile is placed face down and a card (within the pile) with the same color of the book is placed face up on top of the stack.

GOING OUT. Teams must have made a red book and a black book and must also have played all of the cards in both their hand and their foot before they are allowed to go out.

SCORING

After a player goes out, the round has officially ended and scores are tallied according to the chart. When the round ends, any cards still in players' hands are tallied and deducted from the total points of the team's played cards.

Cards/Books	Value
Red books	500 points
Black books	300 points
Wild card books (books made from 2s and Jokers)	1,500 points
Joker	50 points
2	20 points
Ace	20 points
8, 9, 10, Jack, Queen, King	10 points
4, 5, 6, 7	5 points
Black 3	5 points
Red 3	100 points
Going out	100 points

TUNK

Tunk, or Tonk, is a Rummy-type game played with two to four players and a standard deck of fifty-two playing cards. In Tunk, Kings are high, Aces are low, and 2s are wild. The objective of Tunk is to have the fewest points at the end of the round.

SETUP

Before gameplay can begin, a dealer must be selected. Each player draws one card from a shuffled deck. The player with the lowest card becomes the dealer. The dealer shuffles the deck and deals seven cards to each player in a clockwise direction. The rest of the cards form the stock, and they go in the middle of the table. The top card of the stock is then flipped face up and placed beside the stock to form the discard pile.

HOW TO PLAY

Gameplay begins, starting with the player to the left of the dealer and proceeds clockwise. Players then decide to draw a card either from the stock or from the discard pile. To end their turn, they must discard a card.

MELDING. Players can get rid of their cards by melding them into sets and runs. A set is three or more cards of a kind. A run is three or more cards in the same suit in a sequence. Once a player makes a meld, they lay out the cards face up on the table. Players may play onto other players' melds as well as their own.

GOING OUT. When a player gets rid of all of their cards, they are out. Every player then has one more turn to improve their hand. After the round has ended, players tally up their score.

SCORING

A player's unmelded cards count as points. In Tunk, face cards are worth 10 points, numbered cards are worth their pip value (face value), and Aces are worth 1. When a player reaches 100 points, they are out of the game. The last player alive wins.

If a player has 50 points at the first draw, they say "Tunk!" and immediately win the game.

CONQUIAN

Conquian is a two-player Rummy-type game that is played with a standard deck of fifty-two playing cards with the 8s, 9s, and 10s removed to form a forty-card deck. Kings are high, and Aces are low. The objective of Conquian is to be the first to meld eleven cards.

SETUP

Before the game can begin, an initial dealer must be selected. Players pick a random card from a shuffled deck. The player with the lowest card is the dealer. Ties are broken with redraws. The dealer shuffles the deck and deals ten cards one at a time to each player. The remaining cards form the stock and are placed face down in the middle of the table. The top card from the stock is then flipped over to form the discard pile.

HOW TO PLAY

Gameplay begins with the non-dealer. At the start of their turn, each player must select a card from either the stock or the discard pile. The card can be kept only if it can be used to complete a meld. If it can't, it is placed face up in the discard pile. If the player can use the card selected, they must lay the meld down on the table in front of them. They may also play any other melds in their hand. A player's turn ends when they place a card in the discard pile.

MELDING. In Conquian, a meld can consist of either three or four cards of the same rank, or three or more cards of the same suit in sequence.

SCORING

The first player to meld eleven cards wins the game. If the stock runs out, the game ends in a tie.

HISTORY OF RUMMY

Card games are so ingrained in our contemporary society that it might be difficult to imagine them as historical traditions spanning centuries. Your casual game of Cribbage, for instance, has been around since the 1600s. The game Piquet goes back even further to the 1500s. Card games have rich, complicated histories that travel across borders, transcend languages, and intertwine with the histories of other games. Take the game Rummy as an example.

Rummy is such a monumental cornerstone of card gaming that it can't really be thought of as a single game. It is more of a family of games that has evolved into popular variations like Gin, Canasta, and Hand and Foot. While each variation has its own peculiarities, in general a Rummy-type game can be defined as any game that involves a draw and discharge on a player's turn and involves the melding of cards by rank or sequence (see page 63 for more information on melding, drawing, and discharging).

There are two general theories about the creation of Rummy. The first is that the game originated in Mexico around the 1890s. In 1897, game historian R. F. Foster described a game called Conquian in his book *Foster's Complete Hoyle*. The game, played with a Spanish deck of forty cards, possessed similar melding mechanics to modern day Rummy and was apparently very popular in Mexico and the southern United States.

Spain, 1698.

However, Foster noted that he was mystified as to how this game actually got started, which brings us to the second theory of the game's origin.

Some historians argue that Rummy originated in Asia. This belief is based on the fact that one of the qualifications of Rummy—the draw and discharge rule—can be observed in nineteenth-century Chinese card games, particularly Mah-jongg. In 1891, W. H. Wilkinson became enamored by a variation of Mah-jongg named Kun P'ai and created a Western equivalent game called Khanhoo. In spite of the fact that Khanhoo is played with a deck of sixty-two cards, the game is practically the same as modern day Rummy.

Game historian David Parlett further complicates these two theories by merging them and proposing that the Mexican game Conquian is actually the Chinese game Khanhoo, due to the phonetic similarity, and that the game made its way to Mexico via Chinese immigrants. Whether Rummy originated in Asia or Mexico, both theories maintain that the earliest versions of the game were played beginning in the nineteenth century.

By the twentieth century, Rummy had already morphed into various other popular games, including Gin. The book *Culbertson's Card Games Complete*, by Ely Culbertson, describes Gin's history as follows: "The principal fad game, in the years 1941–46, of the United States, Gin Rummy (then called simply Gin) was devised in 1909 by Elwood T. Baker of Brooklyn, N. Y.,

a whist teacher; the name, suggested by Mr. Baker's son, played on the alcoholic affinity of rum and gin; the game was resurgent 1927–30, then dormant until 1940, then adopted by the motion-picture colony and the radio world, who gave it the publicity essential to a fad game." While there is some debate over the accuracy of this origin story, game historians like David Parlett and Dale Armstrong have agreed that it's a strong possibility. Regardless of how the game was created, after Gin gained popularity with a few celebrities in 1930s Hollywood, it was here to stay.

Canasta is one of the few Rummy-based games that has a widely agreed upon origin story. In 1939, Canasta was created by Segundo Santos and Alberto Serrato in Montevideo, Uruguay. Santos was an attorney and an avid Bridge player at the Jockey Club. After becoming dissatisfied with the large amount of time he spent playing Bridge, Santos enlisted his Bridge partner, Serrato, an architech, to help him design a time-efficient game that was as engaging as Bridge. The solution was Canasta, a game rooted in the traditions of Rummy but incorporating less of a luck factor. The game was an instant hit at the Jockey Club and quickly spread northward throughout Latin America, until it finally reached the United States in the 1950s, causing a Canasta craze. Unfortunately, Santos and Serrato never patented the game rules for their casual Jockey Club pastime and did not receive any royalties from the card game boom that Canasta created. Reportedly, a bewildered Santos had this to say about the game's popularity: "I was just trying to get my mind off of Bridge." While the craze has died out since the 1960s, Canasta remains one of Rummy's most popular variations.

These are just a few snippets from Rummy's fascinating and complicated history. These stories paint a picture of the broad evolution of a beloved game, which has been changed and shaped by those who've played it for more than one hundred years.

WHAT'S IN A NAME?

Ever wondered where the name Rummy came from? Well, people believe the word *rummy* derives from the word *rum*. The word *rum* is a British slang word meaning odd, strange, or queer. Perhaps this was the way British players viewed the game, and so they gave it a name to match.

However, another theory says that the name *Rummy* derives from the game Rum Poker. There is an assumption that Rum Poker is the ancestor of every Rummy game played in different parts of the world.

Some gamers also believe the name of the card game comes from the popular liquor. The link between rum and Rummy is pretty much exactly as you'd expect: in early versions of the game, the loser had to buy the winning players the next round of drinks.

TRICK-TAKING GAMES

A trick-taking card game is one in which each player in the game contributes a single card, and the highest-ranking card played wins the round, or "trick." Often played in teams, trick-taking games are perfect for gatherings of friends or family. The basic objective of any trick-taking game is to win more tricks than your opponents.

BEZIQUE

Bezique is a melding and trick-taking game for two players. Bezique uses only the 7s through the Aces (high) from two standard decks of fifty-two playing cards. Cards ranked 2 through 6 should be removed. This game is suitable for ages ten and up. The objective of Bezique is to win the most points through melding and winning tricks that include Aces and 10s.

SETUP

Before gameplay can begin, each player draws a card from a shuffled deck. The player with the highest card becomes the first dealer. Ties are broken by a redraw. The dealer shuffles the deck and deals eight cards to each player. The cards should be dealt in two sets of three and one set of two. The remaining cards form the stock. The top card of the stock is flipped over and placed underneath the stock, sticking out so that everyone can see the suit of the card. The suit of the card is the trump suit for the round. The trump suit ranks higher than any non-trump suit in winning tricks for the rest of the round.

RANKING OF CARDS

In Bezique, cards are ranked from high to low as follows: Ace, 10, King, Queen, Jack, 9, 8, and 7.

HOW TO PLAY

The non-dealer leads the first trick by playing a card from their hand. The dealer then plays a card against it. The highest card in the lead suit wins the trick unless a trump is played. If a trump is played, the highest trump card wins. The winner of the trick picks up the cards that have been played and then has the opportunity to score points by making a meld with any of the cards in their hand.

Melds can be created in any of the following ways, but note that some melds are worth more points than others:

Meld	Value
Double bezique (both Queens of spades and both Jacks of diamonds)	500 points
A sequence of Ace, King, Queen, Jack, and 10 in the trump suit	250 points
Four Aces	100 points
Four Kings	80 points
Four Queens	60 points
A bezique (one Queen of spades and one Jack of diamonds)	40 points
(Chart continues on next page)	

Four Jacks	40 points
A King and Queen in the trump suit	40 points
A King and Queen in a non-trump suit	20 points

Once a meld has been laid on the table, its points are recorded. Throughout the rest of the round, players may still play their melded cards as if they were in their hand. After the winner of the trick decides whether or not to meld, they then draw the top card from the stock. The loser of the trick also draws a card from the stock once the winner has drawn. Each player should have eight cards in their hand. The winner of the last trick then leads the next trick and gameplay continues.

Once the stock is exhausted, no more melds can be made. From this point on, the game turns into a simple trick-taking game where players must follow the lead suit if possible. Players are required to win tricks whenever possible. If a player cannot follow the suit that was led, they must play a trump card (if possible) and win the trick. If a player does not have a card in the suit that was led or a trump card, the player can play any card in their hand.

After the stock runs out, players may keep making tricks but may not form any new melds. Once no more tricks can be made, the game has ended, the dealer position rotates, cards are shuffled, and another round starts.

ADDITIONAL RULES. If a player holds a 7 of the trump suit, they can swap it with the flipped-up trump card placed at the bottom of the stock, but only after winning a trick. Doing this earns a player 10 points.

If the same card is played by both players, the lead card wins the trick.

A card can be used for multiple melds but not twice for the same type of meld.

A player is not able to play a sequence and then later take the points for the trump marriage (King and Queen) contained within that sequence. However, players may lay down the King and Queen meld first and then, on another turn, finish the sequence to get points for both melds.

Some variations of the game allow a player to form a bezique by laying down a King and Queen meld and then laying down four Jacks. The Bezique must be declared on the player's next turn after laying both melds.

A player is awarded 10 points for winning the last trick.

The dealer wins 10 points if the trump suit card they flip up in the beginning is a 7.

SCORING

Points for melds are continually recorded throughout the game.

Each Ace and 10 won in a trick is worth 10 points.

The game is played until one player reaches an agreed upon number of points, such as 500 or 1,000.

BRIDGE

Bridge is a complex trick-taking game for four players in teams of two with a standard deck of fifty-two playing cards. This game is fairly difficult and is best suited for players over the age of thirteen. The objective is to win as many games as possible. A game of bridge is won when one team reaches a score of 100 points. A match of bridge consists of three games and is won by the first team to take two games. In Bridge, Aces are high, and 2s are low. When a trump suit is established, all trump-suited cards will outrank any non-trump-suited card.

SETUP

Before the game begins, an initial dealer must be chosen. Every player is given a card from a shuffled deck, and whoever receives the highest card becomes the first dealer. Ties are broken by a repeated deal. The initial dealer shuffles the deck, and the player to their right cuts it. The dealer then deals thirteen cards to each of the four players one at a time, moving in a clockwise direction.

The dealer position rotates clockwise at the end of each round.

Teammates sit across from each other and work together to make bids and win tricks.

AUCTION

Before the gameplay commences, players enter into an auction for the round's contract and decide to bid, double, redouble, or pass. The auction process starts with the player to the right of the dealer and moves clockwise around the table.

BID. A bid represents the number of tricks a team expects to win along with the trump suit they desire for the round. The minimum bid is seven tricks, and the maximum bid is thirteen. If a player makes a bid of "one heart," they expect to take seven tricks and are asking for hearts to be trump. A bid of "two hearts" is eight tricks with hearts trump, and so on. The rank of suits for bidding purposes from highest to lowest is no trump, spades, hearts, diamonds, and clubs. If a player bids "two hearts" and another player bids "two spades," the bid of "two spades" is considered to be a higher bid. A "no trump" bid is exactly what it sounds like. During that round, no suit is designated as a trump.

DOUBLE. A player can decide to double a bid made by the opposing team if they believe that the other team will not take the number of tricks they bid. By doubling a bid, the player doubles the penalty if the bid is not met but also doubles the payout if the bid is successful.

REDOUBLE. A player can redouble a bid if the original bid was made by their teammate and that bid was then doubled by their opponent. Redoubling quadruples the original bid's payout if successful, but it also quadruples the penalty if unsuccessful.

PASS. If a player passes, they decide not to make a bid, redouble, or double. The auction continues to each player until all players have passed on the highest bid. The highest bid (in terms of suit ranking and number of tricks bid) becomes the contract for the round.

HOW TO PLAY

The player who made the highest bid becomes the declarer, and their team becomes the attackers while the other team becomes the defenders. The teammate of the declarer becomes the dummy. The dummy lays down their cards face up and grouped in suits for all of the other players to see. The dummy hand should be the only hand that is visible. All other players must keep their cards hidden. The dummy does not participate in the round. Instead, the declarer plays for the dummy when it is their turn.

The gameplay officially begins when the declarer lays down the lead card. Going clockwise, the defenders try to outrank the lead card played. A player must play a card of the same suit as the lead card if they have one. If they do not possess cards of the same suit, they may play any of their cards in an attempt to win the trick, including trumps. The winner of the trick places the next lead card, and the gameplay continues until all cards are played. Tricks won should be collected and placed face down on the side of the team who won the trick.

SCORING

Each trick taken over six tricks is worth a certain number of points, depending on the trump suit. A team wins a game after scoring 100 points. The scoreboard for bridge is generally divided into two columns (one for each team) and two rows. The bottom row is for points won by making tricks, while the top row is for bonus and penalty points.

BOTTOM ROW. The following is the point value for tricks taken:

- Tricks taken when diamonds or clubs is trump are worth 20 points.
- Tricks taken when hearts or spades is trump are worth 30 points.

- Tricks taken when there is no trump suit are worth 40 points for the first trick over six and 30 points for each trick thereafter.

TOP ROW.
Bridge contains a lot of bonus points (such as small and grand slams) for teams to earn. A small slam is given to a team who wins twelve tricks. A grand slam is given to a team who wins all thirteen tricks. Bonus and penalty points are affected by whether or not a team is considered to be vulnerable or not vulnerable. A team is vulnerable if they won the last game. Vulnerability increases both bonus and penalty points.

The following are bonus point values for teams that are vulnerable:

- Doubled overtricks are worth 200 points each. Overtricks are bonus points a team receives when they exceed the number of tricks they said they would earn in their contract bid.
- Redoubled overtricks are worth 400 points each.
- Small slams are worth 750 points.
- Grand slams are worth 1,500 points.

The following are bonus point values for teams that are not vulnerable:

- Doubled overtricks are worth 100 points each.
- Redoubled overtricks are worth 200 points each.
- Small slams are worth 500 points.
- Grand slams are worth 1,000 points.

The following are penalty point values for teams that are vulnerable:

- Undertricks cost 100 points each. An undertrick is exactly what it sounds like: not meeting the number of tricks they claimed they would take in their contract bid.
- The first doubled undertrick costs 200 points.
- Each doubled undertrick after the first costs 300 points each.
- The first redoubled undertrick costs 400 points.
- Each redoubled undertrick after the first costs 600 points each.

The following are penalty point values for teams that are not vulnerable:

- Undertricks cost 50 points each.
- The first doubled undertrick costs 100 points.
- Each doubled undertrick after the first costs 200 points each.
- The first redoubled undertrick costs 200 points.

- Each redoubled undertrick after the first costs 400 points each.

Here is a quick reference guide to help you keep track of your scores:

Bottom Row: Point Values for Tricks Taken (over 6 Tricks)			
	Contract	**Doubled**	**Redoubled**
Diamonds/Clubs	20 points	40 points	80 points
Spades/Hearts	30 points	60 points	120 points
No trump (first trick)	40 points	80 points	160 points
No trump (additional tricks)	30 points	60 points	120 points

Top Row: Bonus Points

	Not Vulnerable		Vulnerable	
Each Overtrick	♣ ♦ 20 points	♥ ♠ No Trump 30 points	♣ ♦ 20 points	♥ ♠ No Trump 30 points
Overtrick (doubled)	100 points		200 points	
Overtick (redoubled)	200 points		400 points	
Small Slam	500 points		750 points	
Grand Slam	1000 points		1500 points	

Making Double / Redouble 50 points
Winning 2 of 2 games: 700 points
Winning 2 of 3 games: 500 points

Top Row: Penalty Points

	Not Vulnerable	Vulnerable
Undertrick	50 points	100 points
Undertrick (first) (doubled)	100 points	200 points
Undertrick (additional) (doubled)	200 points	300 points
Undertrick (first) (redoubled)	200 points	400 points
Undertrick (additional) (redoubled)	400 points	600 points

CALIFORNIA JACK

California Jack is a trick-taking game played with four people. It uses a standard deck of fifty-two playing cards. Aces are ranked highest, and 2s are ranked lowest. The objective of California Jack is to get the most tricks, but there are no teams, and players must look out for themselves.

SETUP

Before gameplay can begin, a dealer must be selected. Each player chooses a random card from a shuffled deck. The player with the lowest card becomes the dealer. Ties are broken with repeated drawings. The dealer shuffles the deck and deals six cards to each player one at a time in a clockwise direction. The remaining deck is placed face up to form the stock. The first card showing in the stock establishes which suit will serve as the trump suit for the round.

HOW TO PLAY

The dealer leads and plays the first card. Going clockwise, players must follow suit if they can. If they cannot, they can either play a trump card or cast off a card from another suit. The highest card from the suit that was led wins the trick unless a trump card is played; in that case, the highest trump card that is played wins the trick.

Once a trick is won, the winning player draws one new card from the stock, and then the other players do the same, moving clockwise from the player who won the last trick. Once each player has drawn a new card, the new top card of the stock pile becomes the trump suit, and the winner of the last trick then leads the next trick. The round ends when all cards have been played.

SCORING

Players receive 1 point each for tricks that contain the Ace of the trump suit, the 2 of the trump suit, or the Jack of the trump suit.

The first player to reach 10 points wins the game.

CINCH

Cinch, also called High-Five or Pedro, is a trick-taking game played with four people divided into two teams of two. It uses a standard deck of fifty-two playing cards. The objective of Cinch is to be the first team to get 51 points.

SETUP

Before gameplay can begin, a dealer must be selected. Each player chooses a random card from a shuffled deck. The player with the lowest card becomes the dealer. Ties are broken with repeated drawings. The dealer shuffles the deck and then deals nine cards, three at a time, face down to each player.

RANKING OF CARDS. Cards are ranked Aces high and 2s low.

The 5 of the trump suit is called the right Pedro.

The 5 of the off suit (same color suit as the trump suit) is called the left Pedro. This card is ranked above the 4 of the trump suit.

BIDDING. Starting with the player sitting to the left of the dealer and going clockwise, players look at their cards and make bids on how many points their team will win. Each bid must exceed the previous bid, with 14 as the highest possible bid (see scoring table on the next page). If one player bids 14 before someone else has had a chance to bid, the player who bid 14 automatically wins the bid. Players may choose to pass if they do not want to place a bid.

DISCARD. After one round of bidding, the highest bidder names the trump suit. The other players then discard all of their non-trump-suited cards. Next, and without looking, the dealer deals cards from the stock so that every player has six cards in their hand. Finally, the dealer then looks through the undealt cards remaining in the stock without showing the cards to the other players. The dealer must make sure their own hand contains six cards and should select the best possible cards left in the stock.

HOW TO PLAY

The highest bidder leads the first trick, and, proceeding clockwise, players must follow suit if they can. If players cannot follow suit, they may play a trump card or a non-trump card. The highest-ranking card played wins the trick, and the winner of the trick leads the next round.

SCORING

Teams receive points for winning certain trump cards during the trick-taking portion of the game:

Trump Card	Value
Right Pedro (5 of the trump suit)	5 points
Left Pedro (5 of the off suit)	5 points
Ace, Jack, 10, and 2	1 point each

The final score of each round of gameplay is awarded based on whether the team that won the bidding round achieved the number of points they claimed they would.

If the team that won the bidding round wins at least as many points as they bid, then the score is calculated according to whichever team won the highest number of points. The lower point count is subtracted from the higher point count, and the difference in points is awarded to the winning team.

So, if a team wins the bidding round with a bid of 8 and then goes on to win 8 points to the other team's 6 points, the bidding team is awarded 2 points as their final score for the round.

Conversely, if a team wins the bidding round with a bid of 6 and then goes on to win 6 points to the other team's 8 points, the non-bidding team is awarded a score of 2 points.

Finally, if the team that won the bidding round does not achieve the number of points they claimed they would, that team scores an automatic 0 points while the opposing team scores an automatic 14 points plus the number the bidding team fell short. So, if the bidding team bids 9 points and only makes 6 points, the other team would receive 17 points total.

The first team to reach 51 points wins.

EUCHRE

Euchre is a trick-taking game for four players working in two teams of two. Euchre is played with a deck of twenty-four cards, comprised of the 9, 10, Jack, Queen, King, and Ace taken from each suit of a standard deck of playing cards. The objective of Euchre is to be the first team to win 10 points.

SETUP

Before gameplay can begin, a dealer must be selected. Each player draws one card from a shuffled deck. The player with the lowest card becomes the dealer. The dealer shuffles the deck and then deals, face down, one set of three cards and then one set of two cards to every player. The deal moves clockwise. Each player should receive five cards total.

ESTABLISHING TRUMP. Once the cards have been dealt to each player, the dealer places the remaining four cards face down on the table in a pile and flips over the top card for everyone to see. The player to the left of the dealer then has the option to affirm the flipped-over card as the trump suit. If they wish to affirm the flipped-over card as trump, they order the dealer to pick it up. If this happens, the dealer picks up the card and must then discard any other card from their hand so that they have five cards total. When the dealer discards, they should place the card face down on the stack.

If the player on the dealer's left does not want the flipped-over card to be trump, they simply say "Pass," and then the authority of establishing trump moves to the person on their left.

If each player passes and the authority to establish trump returns to the dealer, the dealer has one of two options. If the dealer wishes for the flipped-over card to become the trump suit, they pick up the card and discard any other card from their hand. If the dealer does not want the card to become trump, they turn the card over.

If the dealer turns the card over, the player to the dealer's left now has the opportunity to declare the trump suit of their choosing, excepting the suit of the card the dealer has just turned over. So, if the dealer just turned over a heart, players may only name diamonds, spades, or clubs as trump.

If the player to the dealer's left does not wish to name a trump suit, they say "Pass" again, and the authority moves to the person on their left just as before. If all three players pass on the opportunity to declare a trump suit, the dealer may also refuse to name a trump. If this happens, all of the cards are collected, a new dealer is chosen, and play begins again.

Some groups choose to play a variation of Euchre that is very politely referred to as "Screw the Dealer." In this version of the game, if the chance to name a trump comes to the dealer for the second time, the dealer must choose a trump suit so that gameplay can continue.

RANKING OF CARDS. In Euchre, Aces are high and 9s are low. However, what makes Euchre unique is that in this game the Jack of the trump suit is called the right bower, and it

is the highest-ranking card. The Jack of the off suit (suit of the same color as the trump suit) is called the left bower and it becomes the second-highest-ranking card after the Jack of the trump suit. All of the cards of the trump suit outrank the other suited cards. So, if hearts is chosen as the trump suit, the Jack of hearts becomes the highest-ranking card, followed by the Jack of diamonds, then the Ace of hearts, the King of hearts, and so on.

TEAMS: ATTACKERS AND DEFENDERS. Teammates sit across from each other. The team who determined the trump suit are called the attackers (or makers), while the other team are called the defenders.

When trump is established, a player may decide to "go alone." If a player decides to go alone (or play by themselves), they must state their intention to do so when they are ordering a trump suit. When a player does this, their teammate must lay their cards face down on the table and abstain from the game. Going alone has possible advantages when it comes to scoring.

HOW TO PLAY

The player to the left of the dealer begins the gameplay by placing a lead card in the center of the table. However, if this player is sitting out a round because their partner has decided to go alone, the player across from the dealer begins play. Going clockwise, every player must follow suit if they can. The player with the highest-ranking card, factoring in the established trump suit, takes the trick. The winner of the trick then plays the lead card for the next round.

SCORING

If the attackers take three or four tricks, they receive 1 point. If they take all five tricks, they receive 2 points.

If the defenders take three or four tricks, they receive 2 points. This is called a euchre. If the defenders take five tricks, they receive 4 points.

If an attacking player decides to go alone and then goes on to take three or four tricks, they receive 2 points. If they take five tricks, they receive 4 points.

Gameplay keeps going until a team earns 10 points.

Points are kept visually for each team by using two number 5 cards of any color, with one card placed over the other. The top card is initially placed face down and is used to progressively reveal pips as the team earns points. Each pip shown counts as 1 point. After 5 points, the top card is flipped up and the cycle begins again.

1 pt

9 pts

VARIATIONS

Euchre is a game with many variations on the number of players, the number of cards, specialty moves, and so on. Some versions, for instance, include the 7s and 8s to form a deck of thirty-two cards.

TWO-PLAYER EUCHRE. Two players may play Euchre with the following method: First, the dealer is chosen with a coin toss. The dealer then deals eight cards to each player. The last three cards are designated as dummy cards. Each player picks up all eight cards and makes the best five-card hand they can, discarding the remaining three. Players can go alone if they decide not to pick up the dummy cards.

AGRAM. Agram is a Euchre variant from the country of Niger. The deck for Agram consists of the 3 through 10 cards plus Aces, with Aces high and 3s low. The player to the left of the dealer leads the first card. Going clockwise, players try to follow suit with a higher-ranked card to win the trick. If they cannot follow suit, they may play any card, but a card not in the lead suit is not ranked. For example, if the lead card is a 7 of clubs, an Ace of diamonds does not outrank it. The winner of the last trick wins the entire game, regardless of how many tricks another player might have won. Only the last trick matters in Agram.

BRITISH EUCHRE. In British Euchre, one card is added to Euchre's usual twenty-four cards: either a Joker or the 2 of spades. The Joker or 2 of spades is called the Benny, and it outranks all other cards. If the Benny is flipped up when deciding trump, the dealer's team automatically becomes the attackers, and the dealer replaces the Benny with one of their own cards.

BUCK EUCHRE. There are no teams in Buck Euchre. Everyone begins the game with 25 points, and players win tricks in order to subtract points (one trick equals 1 point) with the goal being to get to 0. If the attacker (the player who decided trump) wins at least three tricks, they subtract three points from their score and the other players add three points to theirs; if the attacker fails to receive at least three tricks, however, they add 5 points to their own score. Every player must take at least one trick in the game, or else 5 points are added to their score. If a player wins all five tricks, they win the game immediately. If all players pass when deciding trump, there will be no trump in the game and no attacker. A player can also drop out of a round after receiving their cards; this saves them from meeting the one-trick minimum but also prohibits them from subtracting any points.

PEPPER. Pepper, or Big Euchre, follows the rules of regular euchre with a few exceptions. Players receive six cards instead of five. A team wins when they reach 30 points. If a team bids and wins all of the tricks in a round, they receive 12 points; this is called big pepper. All other rules of traditional Euchre apply.

HISTORY OF EUCHRE

As games scholar David Parlett concludes in a definitive article on Euchre: "Euchre derives from the Alsatian game of Jucker . . . It is definitively characterised by the promotion of two Jacks to topmost position as Right and Left Bowers, a feature variously represented or paralleled in late 18th to early 19th century west German games such as Réunion, Bester Bube and Kontraspiel. The promotion of Jacks apparently developed during the 18th century, perhaps as an extension of the promotion of the Jack of Clubs in Loo and Pamphile, perhaps also influenced by the special status of black Aces (or Aces of swords and clubs) in Ombre."

From its European origins, Euchre was likely brought to America by German immigrants. Its first official description in America was written down in the 1845 edition of *Hoyle's Games*. While Euchre's popularity has declined since the 1800s, it still has a strong following in the American Midwest. Countries around the world, however, also indulge in the game, particularly the United Kingdom.

FORTY-FIVE

Forty-Five is a card game for two to five people and played with a standard deck of fifty-two playing cards. Other than a more complicated system for establishing trump and ranking cards, Forty-Five is a traditional trick-taking game where the objective is to win the most tricks.

SETUP

Before gameplay can begin, a dealer must be selected. To do so, players choose a random card from a shuffled deck.

The player with the lowest card becomes the dealer. Ties are broken with repeated drawings. The dealer shuffles the deck and then deals, face down, one set of three cards and then one set of two cards to every player. Once the cards have been dealt to each player, the dealer places the remaining cards face down on the table and flips over the top card on the pile in order to establish trump.

If a player holds the Ace of the trump suit in their hand, they may trade in any of their cards for the card that was flipped over to establish trump. If the flipped-over card is an Ace, then the dealer may trade in any of their cards for that card.

RANKING OF CARDS. The following are the rankings of trump suits from highest to lowest:

- For spades and clubs, the rankings are 5, Jack, Ace of hearts, Ace, King, Queen, 2, 3, 4, 6, 7, 8, 9, and 10.
- For hearts, the ranking is 5, Jack, Ace, King, Queen, 10, 9, 8, 7, 6, 4, 3, and 2.
- For diamonds, the ranking is 5, Jack, Ace of hearts, Ace, King, Queen, 10, 9, 8, 7, 6, 4, 3, and 2.

The following are the rankings of non-trump suits from highest to lowest:

- For spades and clubs, the rankings are King, Queen, Jack, Ace, 2, 3, 4, 5, 6, 7, 8, 9, and 10.
- For diamonds, the ranking is King, Queen, Jack, 10, 9, 8, 7, 6, 5, 4, 3, 2, and Ace.
- For hearts, the ranking is King, Queen, Jack, 10, 9, 8, 7, 6, 5, 4, 3, and 2.

HOW TO PLAY

The player to the left of the dealer begins by placing a lead card in the middle of the table. Going clockwise, every player must follow suit if they can. The player with the highest-ranking card, factoring in the established trump suit, takes the trick. The winner of the trick then plays the lead card for the next trick. If no trump cards are played, the lead suit is highest.

SCORING

Players receive 5 points for taking three or four tricks and 10 points for taking all five tricks. The first player to 45 points wins the game.

GO BOOM

Go Boom is a trick-taking game played with four people. Go Boom uses a standard deck of fifty-two playing cards with Aces high and 2s low. The objective is to be the first player to lose all of their cards. Go Boom does not require selecting a trump suit, which makes this an ideal game for teaching fundamentals of trick taking without incorporating the added layer of difficulty that trump cards can bring to a game.

SETUP

Before gameplay can begin, a dealer must be selected. To do so, players choose a random card from a shuffled deck. The player with the lowest card becomes the dealer. Ties are broken with repeated drawings. The dealer shuffles the deck and then deals, face down, seven cards to each player, going one at a time and moving in a clockwise direction. The remaining cards are used to form a stock in the center of the table.

HOW TO PLAY

The player to the left of the dealer begins by placing a lead card in the center of the table.

Going clockwise, players must follow suit or play a card of the same rank as the card that was led. The highest-ranking card wins the trick, and the winner must then play the first card in the next trick. If two or more cards of the same rank are played, and they are the highest cards played in a trick, the person who played the card first wins the trick.

If a player cannot follow rank or suit, they must draw cards from the stock until they are able to do so. If the stock has run out, and the player still cannot make a play, the player does not make a move for that trick.

Once a player plays their last card, they shout "Boom!" and win the game.

HEARTS

Hearts is a trick-taking game that requires four players and a standard deck of fifty-two playing cards. Aces are ranked highest, and 2s are ranked lowest. The objective of the game is to be the player who scores the fewest points. The game ends when one player reaches 100 points.

SETUP

Before gameplay can begin, a dealer must be selected. Each player draws one card from a shuffled deck. The player with the lowest card becomes the dealer. Ties are broken with repeated drawings. The dealer shuffles the deck and deals thirteen cards to each player, one card at a time and moving in a clockwise direction.

HOW TO PLAY

The player with the 2 of clubs always starts the first hand by leading with that card. Moving to the left, each subsequent player must follow the suit of the card that was led. If a player cannot follow suit, then they may play any other card from their hand. The first card played in a trick becomes the lead suit. So, in the first hand, when the 2 of clubs is played, clubs becomes the highest-ranking suit.

If a player does not have any clubs in their hand on the first trick, that player may throw off any card they wish with the exception of any hearts and the Queen of spades. These cards may not be played until at least the second trick. Whoever wins the first trick then leads the first card of the second trick. All players must follow suit if they can.

SCORING

After all fifty-two cards have been played, players examine the tricks they've won and count up all of the hearts and the Queen of spades. Hearts are worth 1 point each, and the Queen of spades is worth 13 points. All other cards have no point value. Since the object of this game is to score the lowest number of points possible, players want to avoid winning tricks that include any hearts or the Queen of spades.

However, if in the course of a game, a player wins all of the hearts and the Queen of spades, that player "shoots the moon" and receives no points, while all other players receive 26 points.

VARIATIONS

CANCELLATION HEARTS. Cancellation Hearts is a version of Hearts that is best suited for large numbers of players, typically five to eleven. In Cancellation Hearts, two standard decks of fifty-two playing cards are used. Because there are doubles of every card, a new strategy of cancellation emerges. If a pair of cards is played, they cancel each other out in trick ranking but still count as points. So, if both Aces of hearts are played, the next highest card wins the trick, but the winner still takes two points for the hearts. If two pairs of any card are in play, the trick is voided and cards are given to the winner of the next trick. In Cancellation Hearts, a common strategy is to pair up the Queen of spades so that the winner of the trick gets a devastating 26-point addition.

The following illustrates the various deals for each number of players. Depending on the number of players, sometimes a Joker is added to the deck.

In each game that leads with a Joker, the Joker is treated as a 0 of clubs:

- For five players, one Joker is added, twenty-one cards are dealt to each player, and the Joker leads the game.
- For six players, a 2 of clubs and a 2 of diamonds are removed, seventeen cards are dealt to each player, and the remaining 2 of clubs leads the game.
- For seven players, a Joker is added, fifteen cards are dealt to each player, and the Joker leads.
- For eight players, a Joker is added, a 2 of clubs is removed, thirteen cards are dealt to each player, and the Joker leads.
- For nine players, a 2 of clubs, both 2s of diamonds, and both 2s of spades are removed; eleven cards are dealt to each player; and the 2 of clubs leads.
- For ten players, a 2 of clubs, both 2s of diamonds, and a 2 of spades are removed; ten cards are dealt to each player; and the 2 of clubs leads.
- Finally, for eleven players, a 2 of clubs, both 2s of diamonds, and both 2s of spades are removed; nine cards are dealt to each player; and the 2 of clubs leads.

OMNIBUS HEARTS. Omnibus Hearts incorporates the 10 of diamonds. In Omnibus Hearts, if a player wins a trick that contains the 10 of diamonds, 10 points are subtracted from their score. Subsequently, for one to shoot the moon, a player must win all of the hearts, the Queen of spades, and the 10 of diamonds. Shooting the moon in Omnibus Hearts results in either a subtraction of 26 points from a player's score or an addition of 26 points to everybody else's score. The player who successfully shot the moon may choose whichever option best advances their play.

PASSING. Some variations allow for passing. Passing occurs before the 2 of clubs is placed at the beginning of the game, and this creates an extra layer of complexity and allows players to strategize. If the game allows for passing, players will select three cards they would like to get rid of before each turn begins. The direction of the pass changes in cycles of four. On the first turn, players pass their three cards to the person on their left; on the second turn, players pass their three cards to the person on their right; on the third turn, players pass their three cards to the person across from them; and on the fourth turn, no passing occurs. Typically, players want to get rid of high-ranking hearts and the Queen of spades, as those cards will most likely win the player a trick and gain them points.

TWO-PLAYER HEARTS. Two people may play Hearts with an alteration to the deck. In Two-Player Hearts, 3s, 5s, 7s, 9s, Jacks, and Kings are removed from the deck, leaving fourteen cards to be dealt to each player. All general rules remain the same.

IDIOT

Idiot, or Palace, is a trick-taking card game for two to four players. The game requires a standard deck of fifty-two playing cards and is suitable for ages eight and up. In Idiot, 3s are low and Aces are high. The objective of Idiot is to not be the last person holding cards.

SETUP

Before gameplay can begin, a dealer must be selected. Every player draws a card from a shuffled deck. The player with the highest card becomes the first dealer. Ties are broken by a redraw. The dealer then shuffles the deck and deals nine cards to each player. The first three cards are placed face down in front of each player. The next three cards are placed face up on top of the previous three cards. The final three cards constitute each player's hand and are placed face down to the side of the six cards that have already been dealt. These final three cards should be held in the player's hand and should not be shown to any of their opponents. The remaining deck forms the stock in the center of the table.

Before the game starts, every player has the opportunity to exchange any of the cards in their hand with any of the three face-up cards sitting on the table in front of them.

HOW TO PLAY

The player to the left of the dealer begins by placing a card in the center of the table, thereby forming a discard pile. Going clockwise, players must play a card of equal or higher value to the previous card played. Cards of the same rank may be played together. For instance, if a player adds a 5 to the discard pile, the next player may add multiple 6s to the discard pile if they have them.

A player must have at least three cards in their hand at all times. Whenever a player adds a card (or cards) to the discard pile, they must draw a new card (or cards) from the stock to make sure they always have three cards in hand. If a player has more than three cards in their hand after discarding, they do not need to draw any new cards on their next turn.

If a player cannot match or exceed the value of the card that was previously played, and if they don't have a special card (2, 5, or 10), they must take the entire discard pile and add it to their hand.

SPECIAL CARDS

In Idiot, 2s, 5s, and 10s are special cards.

Twos are wild cards. They can be played at any time, and any card can be played on top of a 2. If needed, the player who plays a 2 must then draw a card from the stock in order to return their hand to three cards total. That same player then plays whichever card they please on top of the 2 and will draw again if needed.

If a player plays a 5, the next card played must be equal or lower in rank.

Tens remove the discard pile. When a player plays a 10, the entire discard pile is picked up and moved to the side of the table. The player who played the 10 must then draw a card from the stock pile if needed to return their hand to three cards total. Finally, that same player must then add the first card to the new discard pile. The player may either discard the card they just drew, or they may discard another card from their hand. Once the new discard pile has been created, play resumes.

After the stock is exhausted and a player's hand is empty, the player then moves onto the three flipped-over cards in front of them. After playing the three top cards, the player then blindly plays the three face-down cards. Players can flip over only one face-down card at a time. They must play that card before they can move on to the next card. Once all of their cards are played, they are out. The last person out is the Idiot.

NAPOLEON

Napoleon is a trick-taking game for two or more players. It is played with a standard deck of fifty-two playing cards. Aces are ranked highest and 2s ranked lowest. The objective of Napoleon is to either be the highest bidder and win all of your tricks, or win more tricks than the highest bidder.

SETUP

Before gameplay can begin, a dealer must be selected. To do so, players choose a random card from a shuffled deck. The player with the lowest card becomes the dealer. Ties are broken with repeated drawings. The dealer shuffles the deck and then deals, face down, one set of three cards and one set of two cards to every player. When dealing is finished, each player should hold five cards in their hand.

BIDDING. After cards are received, the bidding process starts with the player to the left of the dealer. Each player looks at their cards and may choose to either bid or pass. A bid is simply the number of tricks a player thinks they can win based on their cards.

The first player to bid five tricks is called Napoleon. If another player wants to bid five tricks, they may do so. They are then called Wellington, as they have outbid the Napoleon bidder. If yet another player wants to bid five tricks, they are then called Blucher, and their bid supersedes the Wellington bid. The bidding process automatically ends once a player makes a Blucher bid. The bidding process ends at the third bid.

The highest bidder plays the first card to start the game. If the highest bidder bid four or fewer tricks, they are referred to as a misere. A misere bidder does not establish a trump suit. If the highest bidder bid all five tricks, they establish a trump suit with the first card they play. So, if a Napoleon, Wellington, or Blucher bidder plays a heart as their first card, then hearts automatically becomes the trump suit for that game.

Once bidding ends, the game becomes a competition between the highest bidder and the other players. The highest bidder wants to earn all of the tricks they claimed they would win, while the other players want to stop them from doing so.

HOW TO PLAY

The highest bidder leads the first card, and play continues clockwise. Players must follow suit or play trump (if trump was established) if they can. If they cannot do either, then the player must discard a card of another suit. Only cards in the lead suit count. The player who plays the highest card wins the trick.

SCORING

If the highest bidder makes their number of bids, they receive that number of points. If a player makes and wins a Napoleon, Wellington, or Blucher bid, however, they receive 10 points.

If the highest bidder fails to make their number of bids, the other players receive what the bidder's points would have been. If the highest bidder bid one trick, then the other players receive 1 point each; if the highest bidder bid two tricks, then the other players receive 2 points each; and so on. If the highest bidder fails to make a Napoleon bid, the other players receive 5 points; if they fail to make a Wellington bid, the other players receive 10 points; and if they fail to make a Blucher bid, the other players receive 20 points.

The first person to score 30 points wins.

OH HELL

Oh Hell, or Estimation, is a trick-taking game for three to seven players. Oh Hell requires a standard deck of fifty-two playing cards. Aces are ranked highest, and 2s are ranked lowest. This game is suitable for ages ten and up. The objective of Oh Hell is to win the exact number of tricks bid.

SETUP

Before gameplay can begin, each player draws a card from a shuffled deck. The player with the highest card becomes the first dealer. Ties are broken by a redraw. The dealer then shuffles the deck and deals cards to each player. For a game of three to five players, the dealer deals ten cards, one at a time, and moving in a clockwise direction. For six players, the dealer deals eight cards. For seven players, the dealer deals seven cards. The remaining deck becomes the stock, which should be placed face down in the center of the table. The top card of the stock is flipped over and placed on top of the pile; this card becomes the trump suit for that round of play.

HOW TO PLAY

Beginning with the player seated to the left of the dealer and going clockwise, each player must make a bid as to how many tricks they believe they can win. Players cannot pass, but they can make a bid of zero if they believe they will not take any tricks. Each player may only bid once, and the dealer must bid last. Players are not required to outbid each other, and the total of all the bids does not have to equal the total number of tricks possible.

Once the bidding process is complete, the player to the left of the dealer leads the first trick, and play then moves clockwise. Players must follow the lead suit if possible. If a player cannot follow suit, they may play a trump card or discard as they see fit. The highest card wins the trick, taking the trump suit into account when applicable.

SCORING

If a player makes the exact number of tricks they bid, they receive 10 points plus the number of tricks bid. So, if a player bids five tricks and then wins exactly five tricks, that player is awarded 15 points.

If a player makes under or over the number of tricks they bid, they receive 0 points.

At any time, a player may ask how many tricks another player has bid, as well as how many tricks another player has won so far.

Gameplay continues indefinitely with the dealer position rotating clockwise after every round. The player with the highest cumulative score at the end of gameplay is declared the winner.

PINOCHLE

Pinochle is a melding and trick-taking game played with two teams of two players. The objective of the game is to be the first team to score 150 or more points. Pinochle is played with forty-eight cards (two sets of 9s through Aces). Cards are ranked as Aces (high), 10s, Kings, Queens, Jacks, and 9s.

SETUP

Before the game begins, an initial dealer must be chosen. Every player is given a card from a shuffled deck, and whoever receives the highest card becomes the first dealer. Ties are broken by a repeated deal. The initial dealer shuffles the deck, and the player to their right cuts it. The dealer then deals twelve cards to each player face down in sets of three, beginning with the player on their left and moving in a clockwise direction.

Once every player has their cards, a round of bidding begins with the player to the left of the dealer and proceeding clockwise. Players make bids based on how many points they believe their team can earn in the coming round of gameplay. The minimum bid is 20, and every player must either increase a previous bid or pass. The bid that forces all other players to pass is the winning bid and becomes the contract for the game. The player who makes the contract then establishes which suit will be trump by declaring the suit of their choice. Before gameplay begins, the team that made the contract trades three cards with each other simultaneously. The person who made the winning bid receives three cards from their teammate. Once they've looked at the cards and incorporated them into their hand, the person who made the winning bid then passes three cards from their hand to their teammate.

HOW TO PLAY

Points are earned in two phases: the melding phase and the trick-taking phase.

MELDING PHASE. A meld is simply a combination of playing cards that helps a player score points. In the melding phase, players examine their hand to see if they contain any of the following combinations. If a player can make any of the combinations below, they must lay their cards down on the table in order to prove their melds to the other players. Cards may be used for creating more than one meld. Points for each team are recorded on a scoring sheet, and then the trick-taking phase begins:

Melds	Description	Value
Trump run	10, Jack, Queen, King, and Ace of the trump suit	15 points
Double trump run	Two trump runs	150 points
Pinochle	Queen of spades and the Jack of diamonds	4 points
Double pinochle	Two pinochles	30 points
Eight Aces	Eight Aces of any suit	100 points
Eight Kings	Eight Kings of any suit	80 points
Eight Queens	Eight Queens of any suit	60 points
Eight Jacks	Eight Jacks of any suit	40 points
Four Aces	Four Aces of any suit	10 points

(Chart continues on next page)

Four Kings	Four Kings of any suit	8 points
Four Queens	Four Queens of any suit	6 points
Four Jacks	Four Jacks of any suit	4 points
Royal marriage	King and Queen of the trump suit	4 points
Common marriage	King and Queen of the non-trump suit	2 points
Nix	A 9 of the trump suit	1 point

TRICK-TAKING PHASE. In this phase, players pick up their previously melded cards and return them to their hand before play begins. Next, each player places a card in the center of the table in the hope of outranking their fellow players and winning each trick. The player who made the contract plays the lead card to begin the game. Going clockwise, players must follow suit of the lead card. If they cannot follow suit, players must play a trump card. If a player cannot follow suit and cannot play a trump card, they may then play any card. Whenever possible, players must always play a higher card than the card that was just laid down.

The following are the possible ways to earn points in the trick-taking phase. In addition to winning tricks that contain these cards, players also earn 1 point for winning the last trick of the game:

Card Type	Value
Ace (of any suit)	1 point
King (of any suit)	1 point
10 (of any suit)	1 point

SCORING

Both teams add up their total score from the melding and trick-taking phases. If the team that made the contract failed to reach the total points they bid, it is called going set, and the number of points they bid is subtracted from their team score. The first team to reach 150 points wins the game. If both teams reach 150 points or more in the same round, the team that made the round's contract wins.

VARIATIONS

CUTTHROAT. Cutthroat is a three-person, no-team version of Pinochle. To begin, fifteen cards are dealt in sets of three cards face down to each player as well as to a "widow" pile seen by no one. Bidding then commences as in Pinochle. The player who makes the bid gets the widow and melds as many cards as they can. Afterward, the player who made the bid discards any three of their unmelded cards. Normal play then proceeds. The point, melding, and trick-taking rules from Pinochle apply.

CHECK. Check is a gambling version of Cutthroat. In addition to the general rules of Cutthroat, players keep track of "checks." Checks are specialty points (separate from Pinochle points) that correspond to a cash value. Players can win checks in the following ways:

- Having a trump run in the melding phase is 1 check.
- Each Ace in tricks won is 1 check.
- Having a roundtable (a marriage in each suit) in the melding phase is 2 checks.
- Playing the hand and losing is a loss of 1 check.
- Having a double marriage (two marriages in same suit) in the melding phase is 1 check.
- Having a double pinochle in the melding phase is 1 check.

- Having double Aces, double Kings, double Queens, or double Jacks in the melding phase is 2 checks.
- Having seven 9s in the melding phase is 5 checks.
- Winning the game is 5 checks.
- The dollar value of a check is determined by the players beforehand. Normally, it is about one dollar.

HISTORY OF PINOCHLE

The modern version of Pinochle originated about 150 years ago and derives from the German game of Binokle (French: Binochle). The name literally means "eyeglasses" or "two eyes." This refers to a myth that the German game was invented from a special deck of cards where the Queen of spades and Jack of diamonds were depicted in profile, revealing one eye each. The pinochle combination of the Queen and Jack therefore gives us two eyes. Pinochle was brought from Europe to America by German immigrants in the nineteenth century.

During the height of World War I, Pinochle was temporarily banned in some US cities due to its German heritage and the anti-German sentiment at the time. It has since regained its popularity and it remains one of the oldest and most beloved games in the world.

PIQUET

Piquet, or PK, is a historic trick-taking game for two players. Piquet uses a standard deck of fifty-two playing cards with the 2s through 6s removed, leaving thirty-two cards. Sevens are low and Aces are high. The objective of Piquet is to win points through creating sets and sequences and by winning tricks.

SETUP

Before gameplay can begin, a dealer must be selected. Players choose a random card from a shuffled deck. The player with the lowest card becomes the dealer. Ties are broken with repeated drawings. The dealer shuffles the deck and then deals twelve cards to each player in sets of three. Once each player has twelve cards, the remaining eight cards are placed in the center of the table and form the stock.

CARD EXCHANGE. The non-dealer can choose to exchange up to five of their cards for cards in the stock. If the non-dealer chooses to exchange cards, the cards that player removes from their hand should be placed off to the side. The dealer can then choose to exchange their cards up to the remaining number of cards left in the stock. So, if the non-dealer chooses to exchange all five of their cards, then the dealer may exchange up to three of their cards for the three cards left in the stock.

If a player has an entire hand with no face cards, this is called a carte blanche. If the player shows their hand before the card exchange takes place, the player is awarded 10 points.

CARD VALUES. These are the card values for the game Piquet:

Card Type	Value
Ace (of any suit)	11 points
10, Jack, Queen, King (of any suit)	10 points
7, 8, 9 (of any suit)	Points correspond to the card's face value

HOW TO PLAY

PHASE 1: SUITS, SEQUENCES, AND SETS. Phase 1 of the game involves scoring points based on certain combinations in a player's hand. Keeping their cards hidden, the non-dealer goes first and declares the highest number of cards they have in the same suit. If the dealer can beat that, they say

"No good"; if they can't, they say "Good"; and if they have the same number of cards in a suit, they say "Equal." If both players have the same number of cards in one suit, then the winner is determined by whichever player's cards have a greater point value. Whichever player's cards have a higher point value is awarded a corresponding number of points.

The player with the highest number of cards in the same suit is awarded points based on the card values. Aces are worth 11 points; Kings, Queens, Jacks, and 10s are worth 10 points; and cards 7 through 9 are worth their face value. If both players have the same number of cards, then the winner is determined by the cards' point value.

After suits are determined, the non-dealer declares how many cards they have in a sequence. A sequence must be made up of three cards or more, and the cards must be of adjacent rank (e.g., 2, 3, 4, etc.). The winner is determined in the same way as above.

If the winner has a sequence of five or more, they earn an additional 10 points.

After sequences are determined, the non-dealer declares how many sets they have. A set must contain either three or four cards of a kind in order to be declared. The player with more sets is awarded 3 points for each set of three and 14 points for each set of four.

PHASE 2: TRICK TAKING. After phase 1 is completed, Piquet becomes a classic trick-taking game. The non-dealer leads on the first trick. The suit that is led must be followed if possible. Whichever player lays down the highest-ranking card wins the trick.

In the trick-taking phase, players win:

- 1 point for leading a trick.
- 1 point for winning a trick that was led by their opponent.
- 1 point for taking the last trick.
- 10 points for taking the most tricks.
- 40 points for taking all of the tricks.

After all of the tricks have been taken and the scores calculated, the cards are shuffled, the dealer position rotates, and a new round begins. The player with the most points after six rounds wins.

PITCH

Pitch, or Setback, is a trick-taking game played with two teams of two players. Pitch uses a standard deck of fifty-two playing cards plus two Jokers, to make a fifty-four-card deck. The objective is to be the first team to reach 52 points. This guide will focus on 10-Point Pitch; popular variations are shown later in this section.

SETUP

Before the game begins, an initial dealer must be chosen. To do so, every player is given a card from a shuffled deck, and whoever receives the highest card becomes the first dealer. Ties are broken by a repeated deal. The initial dealer shuffles the deck and the player to their right cuts it. The dealer then deals nine cards in sets of three to each of the four players in a clockwise direction, starting with the player to their left.

RANKING OF CARDS. Cards are ranked Aces high and 2s low. The Jack of the off suit to the trump (same color suit as the trump suit) is called the Jick, and it is ranked just below the Jack of the trump suit. The Jokers are also considered to be trump cards and are divided between high and low Joker. Jokers should be marked with a pencil or a pen to distinguish which Joker is ranked high and which is ranked low. The Jokers rank above the 10 and below the Jick, with the high Joker ranking above the low Joker.

As an example, if hearts are selected as the trump suit, then the cards will be ranked as follows (from highest to lowest): Ace, King, Queen, Jack, Jick (Jack of diamonds), high Joker, low Joker, 10, 9, 8, 7, 6, 5, 4, 3, 2.

HOW TO PLAY

BIDDING. Bidding begins with the player to the left of the dealer and continues clockwise. During the bidding phase, players bet on how many points they will win in a given game. The minimum bid is 4 points. Players must bid the initial 4 points, bid higher than a previous bid, or pass. A bid must be made, so if every player passes, the dealer must make the initial bid of 4 points. This is called sticking it to the dealer. The player with the highest bid declares the trump suit.

REDRAW. After the bid winner determines which suit is trump, the other players remove all of the non-trump-suited cards from their hands. The bid winner keeps their cards. The discarded cards are then shuffled to form a new deck, and the dealer then deals cards to each bid loser so that they all have six cards. The bid winner then gets the rest of the deck, takes all remaining trump-suited cards for their hand, and then removes all of their non-trump-suited cards.

TRICK TAKING. The bid winner leads the first trick. Going clockwise, players try to play the highest-ranked card to win points. Only trump-suited cards can be played. The winner of the trick takes the lead in the next round. Once a bid loser runs out of trump-suited cards, they fold and gameplay proceeds clockwise with the players who are left in the game.

Once a player runs out of cards, they are out of the game. Gameplay ends when only one player is left.

SCORING

Only trump cards are worth points. Ace, Jack, Jick, high and low Joker, 10, and 2 are each worth 1 point. The 3 card is worth 3 points. The player who played the trump-suited 2 card gets to keep the point even if they lose the trick.

Points are tallied by teams. The first team to reach 52 points wins.

If the bid winner's team does not make the number of points they bid, the number bid is subtracted from their score. For example, if a team wins the bidding round with a bid of 5 points and then only earns 3 points, that team's score would be −2. Teams that have a negative score because they failed to reach their bid are considered to be in the hole.

A team can "shoot the moon" if they bid and win 10 points. A team that "shoots the moon" automatically wins the game.

If both teams reach 52 points at the end of the same round, the team that made the bid for that round wins the game, even if that team had fewer points going in to the round.

Here's a quick reference guide for playing Pitch:

	Card Rank
NEEDED: Fifty-four-card deck (Jokers included) **Four players Pen and paper**	Ace
	King
	Queen
DEAL: Nine cards/player	Jack
	Jick
BASICS: Win tricks with highest-ranking card. Only trump-suited cards played. Two of trump kept by player. Minimum bid 4.	H Joker
	L Joker
	10
	9
	8
WIN: First team to 52 points	7
	6
POINTS:	5
1 point:	4
Ace / Jack / Jick / H Joker	
L Joker / 10 / 2	3
3 points: 3	2

VARIATIONS

Pitch has many variations that differ mainly in how the game is scored. Here are just a few:

OKLAHOMA 10 POINT. In Oklahoma 10 Point, players are initially dealt six cards. The minimum bid a player can make is 1 instead of 4. Other than these differences, the general rules of Pitch apply. Game variations that initially deal six cards are sometimes called Oklahoma style.

CONTWAY 6 POINT. Contway 6 Point, as the name implies, is a 6-point variation of Pitch. In Contway 6 Point, the following cards are worth 1 point: highest trump played, lowest trump played, Jack, Jick, and Joker. Winning the round also results in 1 point. Only one Joker is used in Contway 6 point, and it is ranked below the Jick. During the redraw, players can choose to throw away any number of trump cards. This can be helpful if the bid winner suddenly thinks they bid too high. A team's score can never go negative. Gameplay continues until a team reaches 11 points.

JUNIPER PITCH. Juniper Pitch is a three-team variation of Pitch. Every player is initially dealt eight cards. There is no redraw phase in the game. Instead, all players simply discard two of their cards after the trump suit is determined. Other than this, the general rules of 10-Point Pitch apply.

PRESIDENT

President is a trick-taking game that requires four to seven
players and a standard deck of fifty-two playing cards. If you
have more than seven players, an additional deck of cards is
needed. In President, Aces are high and 3s are low. The objective
of President is to be the first player to get rid of all your cards.

SETUP

Before gameplay can begin, a dealer must be chosen. To do
so, every player draws a card randomly from a shuffled deck.

The player with the lowest card becomes the dealer. Ties are broken with redraws. The **dealer then deals all of** the cards to each player, going one at a **time and moving in a clockwise** direction. It is fine if some players **have more cards than** others at the game's outset.

HOW TO PLAY

The person who received the 3 of clubs plays that card to begin the game. Play then proceeds in a clockwise direction. To place a card, a player must match or outrank the card that was previously played by the player on their right. When a card is matched in rank, the next player is skipped. For example, if the first player lays down the 3 of clubs, and the player to their left lays down a 3 of diamonds, the player to that person's left is then skipped.

A pair of cards outranks any single card. For example, if a Jack is played, the next player can play two 3s to outrank that Jack.

Once a pair is played, another pair of higher ranking is needed to beat that pair.

The same rule holds true for a three of a kind. A three of a kind will beat any pair, and a higher three of a kind is needed in order to beat a three of a kind that has already been played.

If a single 2 is played, the middle pile is removed from the center, and whichever player laid down the 2 begins a new pile. If a player cannot match or outrank the previous card played and also cannot clear the pile by playing a 2, that player must pass.

The first player to get rid of their cards becomes the president. The last person left holding cards at the end of the game becomes the beggar. Once a round is complete, the president shuffles the deck and deals the cards. When the cards have been passed out, the beggar must give the president the highest-ranking card in their hand. In turn, the president will choose a card from their own hand to give back to the beggar. The president then begins the game by playing whatever card they choose.

VARIATIONS

Some variations have a vice president position and a beggar 2 position. The vice president position represents the player who came in second to the president, while the beggar 2 position represents the person who came in second to last. In this case, two cards are exchanged between the president and beggar 1 and one card is exchanged between the vice president and beggar 2. Some games also include Jokers. In these cases, Jokers trump all other cards.

SIXTY-SIX

Sixty-Six is a trick-taking game played with two players and a twenty-four-card deck (9s, 10s, Jacks, Queens, Kings, and Aces). The objective of Sixty-Six is to win the most points by taking tricks.

SETUP

Before gameplay can begin, a dealer must be selected. To do so, players choose a random card from a shuffled deck. The player with the lowest card becomes the dealer. Ties are broken with repeated drawings. The dealer shuffles the deck and deals six cards in groups of three, moving in a clockwise direction. The top card of the remaining cards is flipped over to establish the trump suit for the game. The remaining cards form the stock, which is placed halfway on top of the card used to establish trump.

RANKING OF CARDS. In Sixty-Six, cards are ranked Aces (high), 10s, Kings, Queens, Jacks, and 9s (low).

HOW TO PLAY

The non-dealer begins the gameplay by placing a lead card in the center of the table. The other player must then try to outrank the card if possible with a higher card in the same suit or a trump card. Players are not obligated to follow suit or play a trump card. The player with the highest-ranking trump card or highest-ranking card in the suit led will win the trick.

The winner of the trick draws the top card from the stock, and the loser of the trick draws the next card in the stock. The winner of the last trick then plays the lead card to start the next trick.

After the stock runs out and the trump-suited card is taken, players must follow the suit of the lead card if possible.

SCORING

Players win points the following ways:

Card Type	Value
Royal marriage (King and Queen of the trump suit)	40 points
Common marriage (King and Queen of any non-trump suit)	20 points
Ace (of any suit)	11 points
10 (of any suit)	10 points
(Chart continues on next page)	

King (of any suit)	4 points
Queen (of any suit)	3 points
Jack (of any suit)	2 points

The first person to 66 points wins the round. If all of the tricks are played without someone getting 66 points, the winner of the last trick wins the round. The first person to win seven rounds wins the game.

Here's a quick reference guide for playing Sixty-Six:

	Card Rank
NEEDED: Twenty-four-card deck (Aces down to 9s)	Ace
Two players	10
Pen and paper	
	King
DEAL: 6 cards/player	Queen
	Jack
BASICS: Win tricks with highest-ranking card. Trick winner draws first card. 66 card points = 1 game point.	9
WIN: First player to 7 points	

SPADES

Spades, or Call Bridge, is a four-player card game that combines strategy and luck. Spades uses a standard deck of fifty-two playing cards. Aces are ranked highest, and 2s are ranked lowest. Spades is always the trump suit and will outrank all other cards. The objective of the game is to correctly predict how many tricks you will win per round of gameplay.

SETUP

Before the game begins, an initial dealer must be chosen. To do so, every player is given a card from a shuffled deck, and whoever receives the highest card becomes the first dealer. Ties are broken by a repeated deal. The dealer shuffles the deck, and the player to their right cuts it. The dealer then deals each player thirteen cards one at a time, moving in a clockwise direction.

HOW TO PLAY

After all players have received their cards, bids are made based upon each players' hand. A bid refers to the players' expectation of the number tricks they believe they will win in the round. Each player has thirteen cards, and thus there are thirteen tricks per round. A trick is won by the player who plays the highest-ranking card. Traditionally, all players are required to make a minimum bid of at least one trick.

Gameplay begins after each player has made their bid. The dealer begins the round by playing a card of their choosing. Play then proceeds clockwise, and each player in turn places their card down in an attempt to outrank all other cards in play. A player must only play cards of the same suit as the card that was led. If a player does not possess cards of the same suit, they may play any of their other cards in an attempt to win the trick.

A spade cannot be the first card played in a trick unless the player holds no other suits in their hand, or if spades have been broken. Spades are broken when any player is unable to follow the lead suit and plays a spade onto the trick.

After the round is complete, the winner of the round usually becomes the new dealer. Sometimes players choose to rotate the dealer position clockwise instead of making the winner of the round the new dealer.

SCORING

If a player meets their bid number, 10 points are awarded for each trick that was won. Additionally, 1 point is given for each trick that was won over and above the initial bid. For example, if a player places a bid of five at the start of the round and goes on to win six tricks, the player is given 51 points at the end of the round. Fifty points are given for meeting the initial five bid and 1 point is given for the additional trick. Zero points are given to players who fail to win the number of tricks they bid.

A game usually continues until a player reaches 500 points. The player who reaches 500 points first wins the game.

VARIATIONS

Spades can be played in its basic format, as described above, or players can opt to make the game a little more interesting with the following variations:

TEN FOR 200, OR WHEELS. Some variations of Spades allow players or teams to make a bid of ten for 200 points. In this bid, a single player or a team is saying that they expect to win ten tricks in the round of play. If they do end up winning ten tricks, the player or team receives 200 points. If they fail to make ten tricks, however, they will lose 200 points.

BAGS. Players can opt to make overtricks (tricks won over the initial bid number) into "bags." Instead of winning an additional point, if a player earns 10 bags in the course of a game, they have 100 points deducted from their score. The intention of introducing bags is to cause the players to try to win the exact number of tricks they bid.

FACE UP. In the Face Up variation of Spades, the first four of the thirteen cards dealt for every player are handed out face up. This adds a psychological element to the game as players are left to wonder about the decision-making process behind every move.

JOKER TRUMPS. Players can opt to include the two Jokers in gameplay. If they do so, Jokers become the highest-ranking trump cards. The full-color Joker outranks the one-color Joker, or Jokers can be marked as high and low if they are not easily distinguishable. Both Jokers outrank the Ace of spades. If players choose to include the Jokers, they must remove the 2 of clubs and the 2 of diamonds in order to keep the fifty-two-card count.

NIL. Some variations of Spades allow the player to bid nil for a round. By bidding nil, the player expects to not be able to make any tricks in the game. If the player successfully takes no tricks in the round, they receive 100 points. Players may counterattack a nil bid by playing their lowest cards at the start of the game, possibly forcing the nil bidder to place a higher card and breaking their nil bid.

TEAMS. Instead of every player advocating for themselves, teams may be introduced to create a new playing dynamic. Normally, teams are formed with two people sitting across from each other. At the end of the game, team members' points are tallied together.

HISTORY OF SPADES

Spades was invented around the 1930s in the United States. It has been described as a descendant of the Whist family of games and even characterized as a simpler version of Bridge. Spades became popular all over the world during the 1940s when US soldiers, who had learned to play it in America, began playing the game in Europe during World War II. Because Spades is easily interrupted and relatively simple, it became the perfect card game for soldiers who needed to remain alert in war zones. When the war was over and soldiers returned to the United States, the GI Bill made it possible for many soldiers to attend college. This caused Spades to become incredibly popular at universities across the country, making college students the main players of the game.

WHIST

Whist is a trick-taking game for four players in two teams of two. Whist uses a standard deck of fifty-two playing cards. Aces are ranked highest, and 2s are ranked lowest. The trump suit changes with each deal. The objective of Whist is to be the first team or player to reach 5 points.

SETUP

Before gameplay can begin, a dealer must be chosen. To do so, each player draws a random card from a shuffled deck. The player with the lowest card becomes the dealer. The dealer then shuffles the deck and deals all of the cards one at a time, moving in a clockwise direction. Each player should receive thirteen cards. The last card in the deck is flipped over and placed in front of the dealer. This card is used to establish the trump suit for the round. The dealer may pick up this card after the first trick has been played. Teammates sit across from each other.

HOW TO PLAY

Gameplay begins with the player to the left of the dealer. This player may lead by playing any card of their choosing. Going clockwise, players follow suit if possible and try to outrank the cards played. If a player cannot follow suit, they may then play any of the other cards in their hand. The winner of the trick lays down the starter card of the next trick.

SCORING

After a round of gameplay has been completed, points are rewarded only for the number of tricks won in excess of six. For instance, if a team wins nine tricks, they will receive 3 points. If, however, a team only wins three tricks, they receive 0 points. The first team to win 10 points wins the game.

VARIATION

KNOCKOUT WHIST. Knockout Whist is a variation of Whist for two to seven players, with no teams. After the end of a round, any player who did not win at least one trick is eliminated from play. The objective of this game is to be the last player left standing.

HISTORY OF WHIST

Under the pseudonym Cavendish, Henry Jones, a games scholar from the 1800s, outlined a comprehensive history of Whist in his 1862 book, which had the very succinct title *The Laws and Principles of Whist: Stated and Explained and Its Practice Illustrated on an Original System by Means of Hands Played Completely Through*. In the book, Cavendish mentions that a sixteenth-century Italian poet named Berni included a game called Trionfi in his own book, *Capitolo del Gioco della Primera*. Many believe that Trionfi could be an early ancestor of Whist. Jones also found another ancestor of Whist, Trump (Sometimes called Triumph), in William Shakespeare's *Antony and Cleopatra*. Suffice it to say, Whist is a game that has been around, in one form or another, for quite some time.

HISTORY OF COURT CARDS

The term *court card* refers to a Jack, Queen, or King of any suit included in a standard deck of fifty-two playing cards. The artwork featured on these court cards is very firmly rooted in tradition, and deviation from this familiar look is considered to be a novelty, even today.

But where does this traditional look originate? It is sometimes claimed that the figures of our modern playing court card characters are based on historical personages. For example, you may sometimes hear the suggestion that the four Kings in a deck of playing cards represent Charlemagne, King David, Julius Caesar, and Alexander the Great. Is there any truth to this?

It is certainly the case that there was a period in history where court cards were closely connected with specific personages. There's a long tradition in French playing cards—some of which date all the way back to the sixteenth century—of including famous figures from history and literature on every court card. In this time period, there was a popular trend to associate each court card with a different figure from the past, so often heroes and heroines from antiquity were featured on playing cards. The source material for these popular characters included characters from mythology, theology, and history.

But this practice of assigning identities to the court cards was a relatively late development in the history of playing cards, only beginning in the mid-fifteenth century, which was long after playing cards began to be used throughout Europe. As such, scholars are not able to agree about which characters are represented on which court cards.

So, while it is not possible to say with 100 percent certainty that the King of spades represents King David, below is a list of common characters that were typically used in sixteenth-century French decks. These people represent the most probable ancestors of our current standard deck.

Kings:

- David, biblical king (spades)
- Alexander the Great, Greek leader (clubs)
- Charlemagne, king of the Franks (hearts)
- Julius Caesar, Roman leader (diamonds)

Queens:

- Pallas Athena, the Greek goddess (spades)
- Argine, an anagram of the Latin word *regina*, meaning queen (clubs)
- Judith, from the apocryphal Old Testament book of the same name (hearts)
- Rachel, the wife of the biblical Jacob (diamonds)

Jacks:

- Ogier the Dane, legendary knight of Charlemagne (spades)
- Lancelot, legendary knight of King Arthur (clubs)

- La Hire, French military commander Étienne de Vignolles (hearts)
- Hector, the mythological hero of Troy (diamonds)

Not all these identifications can be certain, nor are they universally accepted. Some argue that Judith was in fact an obscure reference to the wife of Charles VI. Others suggest that Rachel is actually Ragnel, the wife of Sir Gawain of the Round Table, and that Argine should actually be Argeia, a legendary princess from Argo. The Jack of hearts (La Hire) could also be Caesar's comrade Aulus Hirtius, while the Jack of clubs is also sometimes associated with Judas Maccabeus, an important Jewish leader.

In some cases, these names were even printed on the cards themselves. But this tradition is a later development that is unique to France and was not practiced prior to the sixteenth century. Playing cards were in common use in Europe for well over a hundred years before historical and literary figures were identified with the court cards for the first time. And even in the time when this practice became more common, many different identities were used prior to any kind of standardization, with early choices for the Kings also including historical personages like Solomon, Augustus, Clovis, and Constantine.

MODERN TRIBUTE DECKS

Several beautiful modern decks have been produced that commemorate this period of rich card design in sixteenth-century France. Here are three relatively recent examples:

Memento Playing Cards
(Legends Playing Card Co.)

The Memento deck takes its name from the word *memento*, which refers to a keepsake or object kept as a reminder of an event or person or place. Illustrated by Valerio Aversa, it is intended to help us remember and reminisce about the roots of card design. This deck offers a unique interpretation by arranging the characters featured in the deck according to the symbolic meaning sometimes ascribed to the four suits. The historical characters selected to feature on the court cards are in line with the theme each suit traditionally is associated with: spades (death), hearts (love), clubs (knowledge), and diamonds (ambition).

In this deck, the character names are also mentioned on the cards. As an example, the King of spades depicts the biblical king David with a harp and a sword, reflecting his different roles as a warrior, musician, and poet. The Queen of diamonds depicts the biblical figure of Rachel, wife of Jacob, who is seen below holding a flower. Since she was a shepherdess, a lamb is also frequently found in works of art depicting her.

Voltige Playing Cards (Art of Play)

Another example of a modern deck that has been inspired by early French decks is the Voltige deck from Art of Play. This deck derives its name from the French word for *aerial* and is in part a tribute to the art of card flourishing. It was designed as a collaborative project with French designers Henri de Saint Julien and Jacques Denain. Even the colors that this deck is available in give a nod to its French origins, with deep Parisian blue and Moulin Rouge red being the two colors of choice.

The designers drew upon a classic French court card design as their inspiration, giving it their own hand-drawn reinterpretation. The commonly accepted names of characters are actually printed on the cards, as was occasionally done with French designs centuries ago. The French origin of these playing cards has been made into a central theme of the entire deck, and the deck also draws inspiration from Baron Haussmann's nineteenth-century urban-renewal program, which saw new boulevards, parks, and public works emerge as part of the reconstruction of the streets of Paris.

Nouveau Playing Cards
(Bona Fide Playing Cards)

A final example is the series of exquisite Nouveau decks produced by Karin Yan from Bona Fide Playing Cards. She has opted to employ an artistic style that has its origin in the philosophical and artistic Art Nouveau movement, which was popular in France in the late nineteenth century.

To enhance the sense of authenticity, the designer has drawn on actual sculptures and famous artwork depicting these characters as the basis for the designs of her court cards. There are several different theories about the meaning of the four suits, one being that the original French suits represented nobility (spades), clergy (hearts), merchants (diamonds), and commoners and the peasantry (clubs). This is the theory adopted for this deck and used as background for the designer's artwork choices for the four suits in her Nouveau decks.

THE ORIGINS OF TODAY'S COURT CARD ARTWORK

The standard artwork for our modern deck actually owes more of a debt to England than it does to France. Playing cards first arrived in England via mainland Europe, especially Belgium, which had many manufacturing houses of playing cards and produced a large amount of exports. One design from Rouen was especially popular and influential. But even in England there was a real diversity of designs due to the large number of different printers that eventually sprang up there. But this all changed with the success of printer Thomas de la Rue, who developed new printing techniques that enabled him to increase productivity and reduce the cost of playing cards. This eventually enabled him to gain somewhat of a monopoly on the playing card industry. Independent designers and producers were absorbed under his leadership, and his work also led to the standardization of playing card design in England. The designs of de la Rue's court cards did receive some modernization at the hands of Reynolds and Sons in 1840 and again by Charles Goodall in 1860. But it is the de la Rue design, inherited and updated by Goodall, that is effectively the design still used today.

It is difficult to establish with any degree of certainty the significance of the precise details of the characters, clothing, and accessories seen in court cards today. Why does the Jack of clubs carry a leaf? Why do Queens carry a flower? Why is the

King of hearts (commonly referred to as the Suicide King due to the position of his sword) the only one not to have a moustache? Why is the King of diamonds the only King who bears an axe instead of a sword? Some of these details may be corruptions of royal accessories like scepters and arrows, but we can't be sure.

Rather than see them as deliberate choices with a singular and clear origin, it is more likely that modern playing cards simply bear the marks of the different cultures that they passed through in order to arrive at the present day. What we see in our Kings, Queens, and Jacks today owes just as much of a debt to fifteenth-century rural Germany as it does to sixteenth-century France and nineteenth-century England. What remains in our modern deck today are faint remnants of dust from the past, which have a permanent place in standard playing card artwork even while their original significance has long been lost. So next time you're admiring a court card, think about the hundreds of years of evolution through multiple countries that played a role in shaping it into what it looks like today.

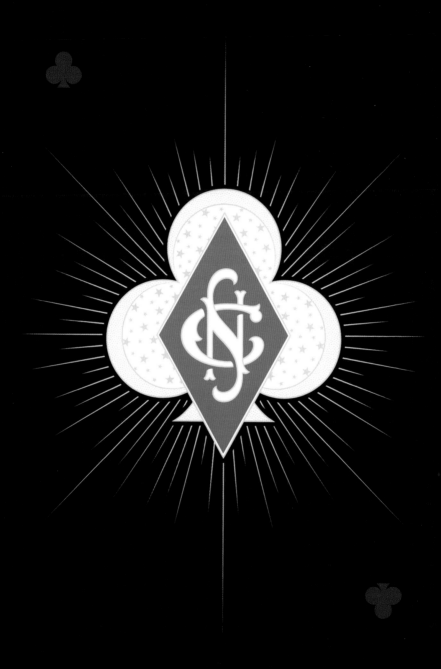

GAMBLING & CASINO GAMES

The games in this section involve betting, and some of these games, such as Baccarat, are popular in casinos around the world. However, many players get just as much enjoyment from playing these games at home with bottle caps, pennies, candy, or other small items you can find in quantity around the house.

Also note that house rules can vary widely in both friendly games and casino games, so be sure to verify house rules if you are playing for real money.

BACCARAT

Originating in mid-nineteenth-century France, Baccarat, or Punto Banco, is a casino-type game that requires no technical skill to play. Often played for high stakes, Baccarat can be found in the big-money sections of most European and Nevada casinos. The objective of Baccarat is to bet on the hand you believe will be as close as possible or equal to 9.

RANKING OF CARDS

In Baccarat, Aces are low, 10s and face cards are worth 0, and all other cards are worth their pip (or face) value.

HOW TO PLAY

To begin the game, players must simply walk up to a Baccarat table and place a bet based on one of three outcomes: your hand winning, the banker's hand winning, or a tie. To play Baccarat at home, you'll need two players: one person to act as the "house" and one person to act as the "player."

PLAYER. If you bet on your hand winning and then you win, you will receive a payout of 1:1. In this scenario, the house has a 1.24 percent edge over the player.

BANKER. If you bet on the banker's hand winning and the banker's hand does win, you will receive a payout of 1:1. You will, however, have to pay the house a 5 percent commission on your winnings from the banker's hands. In this scenario, the house has a 1.06 percent edge over the player.

TIE. If you bet on a tie and win, you will receive a payout of 8:1 (sometimes 9:1). The house, however, has a 14.36 percent edge over the player in this scenario.

When bets are made, the dealer will draw two or three cards for the player's and banker's hand. Whichever hand gets closer to 9 wins.

If a hand exceeds 10, then 10 is subtracted from the hand. For example, a hand of an 8 and a 5 is 13, so a player's total hand value is 3. Neither the dealer nor the player decides if a third card is drawn. Instead, the rules of Baccarat determine this, as illustrated by the following chart.

Player

Having	Next Move
1-2-3-4-5-10	Draws a card
6-7	Stands
8-9	Natural (Banker cannot draw)

Banker

When Banker's first two cards total:	Banker draws when Player's third card is:	Banker stands when Player's third card is:
3	1-2-3-4-5-6-7-9-10	8
4	2-3-4-5-6-7	1-8-9-10
5	4-5-6-7	1-2-3-8-9-10
6	6-7	1-2-3-4-5-8-9-10
7	Stands	
8-9	Natural (Player cannot draw)	

BLACKJACK

Blackjack, or Twenty-One, is a casino-type game where players bet against the dealer for hands as close to 21 as possible without going over.

RANKING OF CARDS

Cards from 2 to 10 are worth their pip (or face) value. Face cards are worth 10. Aces are worth 11 or 1, depending on which is more advantageous to the hand.

SETUP

At the beginning of the game, the dealer shuffles the pack of cards (normally, more than one pack is used) and selects a random player to cut the deck. After the deck is cut, a plastic insert is placed randomly in the deck to designate a reshuffle point. This limits the ability of card counters and makes it more difficult to beat the dealer.

Players then make their bets on the round. The dealer deals one card face up to everyone, including themselves. Next, the dealer deals one card face up to all of the players and one card face down for their own hand.

POSSIBLE OUTCOMES

WINNING. If the player's hand is closer to 21 than the dealer's, they win an amount equal to their bet. If their hand is equal to 21, it is called a blackjack or a natural, and they automatically win 3:2 as long as the dealer does not also have a blackjack. If both the player and the dealer have a blackjack, this is called a push, and no exchange of bets is made.

LOSING. If the dealer's hand is closer to 21 than the player's, the player loses their entire bet. If the player's hand goes over 21 after a hit, it is called a bust, and they automatically lose their bet, regardless of whether or not the dealer also busts.

PUSHING. If the player's hand and the dealer's hand are equal, the player does not win or lose anything.

HOW TO PLAY

Players always go first in a game of Blackjack, before the dealer reveals their face-down card.

However, before a player begins official play, they may opt to do one of two things: They can buy insurance or surrender. A player may buy insurance if they believe the dealer has a blackjack. Insurance pays 2:1. If a player makes an insurance bet that is half their original wager, and then the dealer hits a natural blackjack, they will get back double their insurance bet, which equals their original bet. Insurance should be bought only when the dealer's face-up card is a 10, a face card, or an Ace. Additionally, a player may surrender their hand if they are confident that they will lose. Surrendering gives the player back half of their bet while the other half is given to the dealer.

A player may choose to buy insurance or surrender, but they can also choose to do neither, and gameplay will continue as normal.

Starting with the player to the dealer's left, each player tries to get their hand closer to 21 than the dealer's without going over or equal to the dealer's. This can be done by hitting, standing, splitting, and doubling down.

HITTING. A player can choose to hit, which means they will be given an additional card from the deck. Hitting can be signaled by saying "Hit" or tapping the table.

STANDING. A player can choose to stand and keep the original cards they've been dealt. Standing is signaled by a player waving a flat hand across their cards.

SPLITTING. A player can decide to split their cards only if the cards originally dealt to them are a pair. Splitting turns the pair of cards into two individual hands, each with its own bet that is equal to the player's initial bet. The dealer then deals the player two additional cards to complete each hand. The player then has the option to hit, stand, split, or double down on each of their hands separately.

DOUBLING DOWN. If a player is confident in their hand, they can decide to double down by doubling their initial bet. After the initial bet is made, the dealer gives the player one more card. After that, the player must stand.

BASIC STRATEGY

While the casino almost always has the advantage, players can adapt to a mathematically proven strategy, known as basic strategy, to increase their chances of winning at Blackjack. Here are a few general rules of basic strategy:

- Never take insurance. For the most part, it is not worthwhile. If the dealer does have a blackjack, you are better off taking a loss.
- Always double down if your initial cards are worth 9, 10, or 11. In this scenario, an additional card will only help you get closer to 21, and you cannot go over 21, which is known as going bust.
- Always opt to stand if your hand is 12 or greater and the dealer's up card is 2 through 6. In this scenario, the dealer

will hit, and hopefully they will either get a hand with a lower value than yours or go bust.

- Always take a hit if the dealer's up card is 7 through an Ace, and your hand is 12, 13, or 14, or an Ace plus 2 through 6. If the dealer has a 7 through an Ace, they are in an advantageous position, and it is better to try your luck with an additional card.
- Always split if you have a pair of 2s, 3s, 6s, 7s, 8s, or 9s, and the dealer's up card is 2 through 6.
- Always split if you have two Aces.

BOORAY

Booray, or Bourré, is a casino-type game for four or more players played with a standard deck of fifty-two playing cards. Aces are ranked highest, and 2s are ranked lowest. The objective of Booray is to win the most tricks out of five rounds.

SETUP

Players start by placing an ante, or a beginning bet, in order to form a pot.

Before gameplay can begin, a dealer must be selected. To do so, players choose a random card from a shuffled deck. The player with the lowest card becomes the dealer. Ties are broken with repeated drawings. The dealer shuffles the deck and then deals five cards face down, one at a time, to every player, moving in a clockwise direction. The next card from the deck is flipped over to establish the trump suit for the game.

Players then look at their cards and decide if they wish to continue playing. If a player folds, they forfeit their ante and leave the game. If they intend to continue playing, an additional bet may ensue. Those who continue playing may replace up to four cards in their hand with new cards dealt by the dealer. They may also choose to keep their hand as is.

HOW TO PLAY

The player to the left of the dealer begins gameplay by placing a lead card in the center of the table. Going clockwise, players must follow suit if they can, and they must play their highest card whenever possible. If they can't follow suit, they can play a trump card or any other card. The highest card wins the trick, and the winner of each trick leads the next trick.

The player with the most tricks wins the pot.

FAN TAN

Fan Tan, also known as Sevens or Play-or-Pay, is a casino-type game suitable for three to eight players. The game requires one standard deck of fifty-two playing cards and one set of poker chips for each player. In Fan Tan, Kings are ranked highest and Aces are ranked lowest. The objective is to be the first player to get rid of all of your cards. The player who wins the round is awarded the pot of chips.

SETUP

Each player places one poker chip in the middle of the gameplay to serve as the game's ante.

Before gameplay can begin, a dealer must be selected. To do so, players choose a random card from a shuffled deck. The player with the lowest card becomes the dealer. Ties are broken with repeated drawings. The dealer shuffles the deck and deals all of the cards, one at a time, moving in a clockwise direction. It is okay for some players to have more cards than others at the game's outset; however, it is customary for players with fewer cards to ante one additional chip.

HOW TO PLAY

The player to the left of the dealer begins by placing a 7 in the center of the table if they can. The game continues clockwise. Players either play a 7 to start a new pile or build upon an existing pile that was created using a 7. Only one card can be played per turn.

If a player opts to build on an existing pile, they must play a card of the same suit as the 7 in their chosen pile, and the card must either be one rank above or below the card they want to play on. For example, if the 7 of clubs has been played, another player can place the 6 of clubs on it, while another player can play the 5 of clubs on the 6 of clubs, and so on.

Players must play a card whenever they can. If a player cannot play any cards, they must add one poker chip to the pot. Play then continues clockwise.

The first player to get rid of all of their cards wins the game. The other players must then contribute one additional chip to the pot for every card left in their hand. So, if a player has three cards left at the end of the game, they must add three additional chips to the pot.

GUTS

Guts is a two-card variant of poker. The game is played with a standard deck of fifty-two playing cards and is suitable for two or more players. In Guts, Aces are ranked highest, and 2s are ranked lowest. The objective is to win the pot by having the highest hand.

SETUP

Players start by placing an ante, or initial bet, into the pot.

Before gameplay can begin, a dealer must be selected. To do so, players choose a random card from a shuffled deck.

The player with the lowest card becomes the dealer. Ties are broken with repeated drawings. The dealer shuffles the deck and then deals two cards face down, one at a time, to every player, moving in a clockwise direction.

Players then look at their hand and decide if they would like to continue playing. If they decide to forfeit their hand, their ante is returned to them.

RANKING OF HANDS. Because players receive only two cards in Guts, the highest pair outranks other hands (e.g., a pair of Aces is the highest-ranked hand). If there are no pairs, the highest card outranks other hands. If two people have the same high card, the highest second card wins.

HOW TO PLAY

After players declare their intention to continue playing, all cards are flipped over. The best hand wins the pot. If there is a tie for the best hand, the pot is shared among the winners equally.

IN-BETWEEN

In-Between is a casino-type game played with two or more players. In-Between (also called Acey-Deucey or Yablon) uses a standard deck of fifty-two playing cards. Aces are ranked highest, and 2s are ranked lowest. In this game, you wager bets on a card's rank being in between two previously drawn cards.

SETUP

To start, all players place a minimum bet into the pot.

Before gameplay can begin, a dealer must be selected. To do so, players choose a random card from a shuffled deck. The player with the lowest card becomes the dealer. Ties are broken with repeated drawings. The dealer shuffles the deck and then places two cards face up and a few inches apart in the center of the table.

HOW TO PLAY

After the first two cards have been dealt, and beginning with the player to the left of the dealer, each player takes a turn placing an additional bet in the amount of their choosing. The bet may be as low as one chip or as high as the entire pot. After the individual bet has been placed, the dealer then places a third card in between the previously drawn cards and turns it face up. If the third card's rank is in between the other cards, the betting player wins 2:1 from the pot. If the third card is not in between the other two cards, or if it is of the same rank as either of the other cards, the bet made is added to the pot and play passes to the next player.

The dealer then removes all three cards from the gameplay area and begins the process again, flipping over two cards and waiting for the next player to place a bet before flipping over a third card.

This means that the Ace and 2 are the best combination for betting. This also means that if the two cards placed face up are in consecutive order, the betting player automatically loses.

If the two face-up cards are of the same rank, the betting player automatically wins two chips from the pot.

If the pot runs out of chips, all players place another minimum amount in it.

VARIATION

RED DOG. In Red Dog, players receive five cards from the dealer. Players make their bets, then the dealer draws an additional card and places it in the middle of the table. If players have a card that is of the same suit and of a higher rank than the card drawn, they receive 2:1 odds.

MICHIGAN

Michigan is a casino-type game for three or more players. The game requires a standard deck of fifty-two playing cards along with an additional Ace of hearts, King of clubs, Queen of diamonds, and Jack of spades taken from another deck and kept separate. In Michigan, Aces are ranked highest and 2s are ranked lowest. The objective of the game is to win boodle, or poker chips, off the antes placed in the middle of the table, and to be the first player to get rid of all of your cards.

SETUP

Before gameplay can begin, a dealer must be selected. To do so, players choose a random card from a shuffled deck. The player with the lowest card becomes the dealer. Ties are broken with repeated drawings. The dealer sets aside the Ace of hearts, King of clubs, Queen of diamonds, and Jack of spades from the additional deck, then shuffles the main deck and deals all of the cards face down, one at a time and moving in a clockwise direction. While doing so, the dealer must also deal a widowed hand—a spare hand that is placed to the right of the dealer and seen by no one. It is okay for some players to have more cards than others at the game's outset.

ANTES. The additional Ace of hearts, King of clubs, Queen of diamonds, and Jack of spades are placed face up in the middle of the table. These are called the antes. Each player other than the dealer must place one poker chip on each of the antes. The dealer must place two poker chips.

HOW TO PLAY

Before play begins, the dealer has the option to switch hands with the widowed hand, but they may not look at the widowed hand before they make this decision. If the dealer chooses not to take the widowed hand, the other players may then bid for the right to replace their own hands with the widowed hand. Whoever places the highest bid wins the hand and must pay the dealer directly.

The player to the left of the dealer begins gameplay, and the game then proceeds in a clockwise direction. To start, the first player may lead with any suit, but they must play the lowest card in whichever suit they play. Whichever player has the next card in the sequence must play next. So, if the player to the left of the dealer plays a 6 of hearts, whichever player has the 7 of hearts must play that card next, no matter where they are seated.

All cards must be played in sequence. If no player can continue a sequence, play stops, and the player who laid down the last card begins a new sequence. They can play a card of any suit, but once again they must play the lowest card in whichever suit they choose. The same suit cannot be played twice in a row after a stop. When a player is able to play a card that matches one of the ante cards (Ace of hearts, King of clubs, Queen of diamonds, or Jack of spades), they then take the chips off of the corresponding ante card in the center of the table.

Any chips that remain on the Ante cards when a hand is finished should remain on the card until they are won in a later hand. When a player runs out of cards, the game ends and each player must pay the winner a number of chips equal to the number of cards remaining in their hand.

RED OR BLACK

Red or Black is a betting game for two or more people. The game uses a standard deck of fifty-two playing cards, and the objective is to guess the correct color of the drawn card.

SETUP

Before gameplay can begin, a dealer must be selected. To do so, players choose a random card from a shuffled deck. The player with the lowest card becomes the dealer. Ties are broken with repeated drawings. The dealer then shuffles the deck. All players place a minimum bet into the pot.

HOW TO PLAY

In Red or Black, play is only between two people with players rotating after each round.

BETTING. For betting in Red or Black, the non-dealer places a minimum bet on the table while the dealer places five cards face down on the table. The non-dealer says either "red" or "black" and the dealer then turns the five cards face up. If three or more cards are the color guessed, the non-dealer collects 2:1 from the pot. If three or more cards are not the color guessed, the non-dealer loses the bet and the minimum bet goes into the pot.

After all players have played a round, the dealer position is rotated one seat to the left.

SEVEN-CARD STUD

Seven-Card Stud is a casino-type poker game where the objective is to win the best hand out of a group of players. Players are given seven cards (hence the name). They then try to make the best five-card hand out of the seven cards while betting against the other hands in play. Seven-Card Stud is played with a standard deck of fifty-two playing cards. Aces are ranked highest, and 2s are ranked lowest.

SETUP

To begin a game of Seven-Card Stud, a dealer must first be chosen. To do so, a random player deals cards face up from a shuffled deck to each person in the game. The first player to draw an Ace becomes the dealer for the round.

RANKING OF HANDS FROM LOWEST TO HIGHEST

Hand	Description
High card	If no one has at least a pair, the highest card wins
One pair	Any two cards of the same rank (two Jacks, for example)
Two pairs	Two sets of two cards, each of the same rank
Three of a kind	Any three cards of the same rank (three Jacks, for example)
Straight	Five cards in sequence that are not of the same suit
Flush	Any five cards that are of the same suit
Full house	Three of a kind and one pair; if multiple players have a full house, the player with the highest-ranking three of a kind wins
Four of a kind	Any four cards of the same rank (four Jacks, for example)
Straight flush	Five cards in sequence that are also of the same suit
Royal flush	An Ace, King, Queen, Jack, and 10, all of the same suit

HOW TO PLAY

The game begins with everyone placing an initial bet into the pot. For casual games, this is normally a dollar or two, or a piece of candy. Play then proceeds through the following five rounds: round 1, fourth street, fifth street, sixth street, and river.

After the initial bet has been added to the pot, and after the dealer deals three cards to each player (see round 1), players have five moves they can make. They can fold, check, bet, call, or raise.

FOLD. To fold, players surrender their hand, losing whatever bets they may have already placed in the pot.

CHECK. To check, players pass on the option to make a bet. Checks can happen only if no bets have been made in the round thus far.

BET. To bet, players put any amount of money they think matches the worth of their hand into the pot. The first bet determines the stakes of the round.

CALL. To call, players make a bet equal to the amount of the previous bet.

RAISE. To raise, players make a bet larger than the amount of the previous bet.

ROUND 1. After each player has made their initial bet, the dealer then deals two cards face down to every player, one at a time and moving in a clockwise direction. These cards are called the "holes," and they remain face down until the "river." Then the dealer deals one card face up to every player. This card is called the "door." After the door is given to each player, a round of betting occurs called the "bring-in." The bring-in begins with the player who has the lowest-valued door card and proceeds clockwise to their left. The first player must place a bet, which can be the lowest bet agreed on by the

table (two chips, one bottle cap, etc.). Each subsequent player may choose to raise, check, call, or fold.

Ties for the lowest-valued card are broken by ranking the suits alphabetically by name, with clubs being the highest and spades being the lowest (e.g., the 2 of clubs outranks the 2 of spades, so the player with the 2 of spades would bet first). At any round of betting, players can decide to fold their hand, but they forfeit any bets they previously added to the pot.

FOURTH STREET. All players still in the hand after round 1 receive a fourth card that is also turned face up. Another round of betting occurs. The player whose face-up cards produce the best poker hand bids first. The initial bidder from this point on may choose to check, which means they are still in the hand but not betting, or they can choose to raise or fold.

If no players are able to produce a poker hand of any ranking after the fourth street card is dealt, then the player who received the highest fourth street card bids first.

FIFTH STREET. The dealer deals a fifth card face up to any remaining players. Another round of betting occurs, starting with the player who has the highest hand and proceeding clockwise to their left. If players have hands of equal rank, the player who received the highest fifth street card bets first.

SIXTH STREET. The dealer deals a sixth card face up to any remaining players. A round of betting occurs, starting with the player who has the highest hand and proceeding clockwise to their left. Players may again choose to call, raise, or fold. If players have hands of equal rank, the player who received the highest sixth street card bets first.

RIVER. In the final round, called the "river," the dealer deals a seventh final card face down to any remaining players.

Each player then views their three face-down cards and makes the best five-card hand they can out of their seven cards without revealing it to the other players. A round of betting occurs, starting with the player who has the highest-ranking visible hand and proceeding clockwise to their left. Once the round of betting ends, the remaining players reveal their hands and the pot goes to the player with the highest-ranking hand.

VARIATIONS

ANACONDA. In Anaconda, cards are not passed out in rounds. Instead, every player is given seven cards at the start of the game. Each player looks at their cards and then passes three cards to the player to their left. Next, a round of betting occurs. Then, players pass two cards from their hand to the player on their left. Another round of betting occurs. Finally, players pass one last card to their left and a final round of betting takes place. As always, the best hand wins.

BASEBALL POKER. In Baseball Poker, 3s and 9s are wild. Additionally, if a player is given a 4, they receive another card. These rules allow for a possible five of a kind, a hand that trumps a royal flush. The game highlights these cards because of their relevance to the game of baseball: three strikes, four balls, and nine innings.

BLIND MAN'S BLUFF. In Blind Man's Bluff, players hold one of the hole cards up to their forehead, facing out. This means everyone can see one hole card for each of their opponents, but they cannot see their own. A more casual version of this game allows players to simply place one card on their forehead and then place bets based on who has the highest card. Suit rankings are determined with each game.

CINCINNATI POKER. The most popular version of Cincinnati Poker is to deal four hole cards to each player with four community cards.

LET IT RIDE. Let It Ride has many of the same rules as classic Seven-Card Stud, with two main differences: Players may reduce their wager, and gameplay stops on fifth street. Players can choose to reduce their wager by one-third after they are given their initial two cards and after the first community card is dealt. Players are allowed to look at their initial two cards but may not show their cards to any of the other players. Let It Ride also has set payouts: A royal flush pays 1,000:1. A straight flush pays 200:1. A four of a kind pays 50:1. A full house pays 11:1. A flush pays 8:1. A straight pays 5:1. A three of a kind pays 3:1. Two pairs pay 2:1. A pair of 10s or better pays 1:1.

RAZZ. Razz is a lowball poker variant of Seven-Card Stud. All general rules from basic Seven-Card Stud apply here except that the objective of this game is to have the lowest hand at the end of play. In lowball poker, straights, flushes, and suits are irrelevant. The ranking of lowball hands are as follows (from highest to lowest):

Ace, 2, 3, 4, 5	Ace, 3, 4, 5, 6	Ace, 2, 4, 5, 7
Ace, 2, 3, 4, 6	2, 3, 4, 5, 6	Ace, 3, 4, 5, 7
Ace, 2, 3, 5, 6	Ace, 2, 3, 4, 7	
Ace, 2, 4, 5, 6	Ace, 2, 3, 5, 7	

SEVEN-CARD HIGH AND LOW. In Seven-Card High and Low, all general rules from basic Seven-Card Stud apply except that at the end of the game, players make two hands out of their seven cards, one high hand and one low hand. The pot is split between the highest and lowest hand. If the pot cannot be split evenly, the odd chip goes to the winner who has the highest hand.

HISTORY OF POKER

While the history of Poker is by no means definitive, many games scholars point to the French game Poque and the Persian game As-Nas as possible early inspirations. What is certain is that the game of Poker first became popular in the American South during the 1830s. Throughout this time, gambling riverboats began spreading the game up and down the Mississippi River and around the city of New Orleans. Con artists of the era were often referred to as "pokes" by disgruntled players, and they were known to use the game as a means of relieving rich tourists of their money.

Originating within the American Midwest, Seven-Card Stud didn't appear until the mid-nineteenth century. While Poker was spread on riverboats, Seven-Card Stud was largely spread by the US military. After World War II, the game became a staple at most casinos and continued to grow in popularity until Texas Hold 'Em and other community card games overtook the gambling scene in the 1980s.

TEXAS HOLD 'EM

Texas Hold 'Em is a casino-type game where the objective is to create the best hand out of a group of players. Players are initially given two cards, called "hole cards," that they hold throughout the game (hence the name). They then try to make the best five-card hand out of their initial hole cards and five additional community cards shared by all players.

RANKING OF HANDS FROM LOWEST TO HIGHEST

Hand	Description
High card	If no one has a pair, the highest card wins
One pair	Any two cards of the same rank (two Jacks, for example)
Two pairs	Two sets of two cards, each of the same rank
Three of a kind	Any three cards of the same rank (three Jacks, for example)
Straight	Five cards in sequence that are not of the same suit

Flush	Any five cards that are of the same suit
Full house	Three of a kind and one pair; if multiple players have a full house, the player with the highest-ranking three of a kind wins
Four of a kind	Any four cards of the same rank (four Jacks, for example)
Straight flush	Five cards in sequence that are also of the same suit
Royal flush	An Ace, King, Queen, Jack, and 10, all of the same suit

SETUP

In Texas Hold 'Em, there are three roles that rotate clockwise after each game: dealer, left blind, and right blind.

DEALER. Before the game begins, an initial dealer must be chosen. To do so, every player is given a card from a shuffled deck, and whoever receives the highest card becomes the first dealer. Ties are broken by a repeated deal. The dealer is given a token or button to signify their role. The initial dealer shuffles the deck and the player to their left cuts it. The dealer will then advance the steps of play as discussed in the "How to Play" section below.

LEFT BLIND. The left blind is the player seated to the left of the dealer. This player makes an initial bet before anybody gets their cards.

RIGHT BLIND. The right blind is the player seated to the left of the left blind. They must double the bet of the left blind.

HOW TO PLAY

After the blinds have added to the pot, the dealer deals two cards face down to each player. In Texas Hold 'Em, players have five moves they can make with each round: fold, check, bet, call, and raise.

FOLD. To fold, players surrender their hand, losing whatever bets they may have already placed in the pot.

CHECK. To check, players pass on the option to make a bet. Checks can happen only if no bets have been made in the round thus far.

BET. To bet, players put any amount of money they think matches the worth of their hand into the pot. The first bet determines the stakes of the round.

CALL. To call, players make a bet equal to the amount of the previous bet.

RAISE. To raise, players make a bet larger than the amount of the previous bet.

ROUNDS

In Texas Hold 'Em, there are five rounds per game: pre-flop, flop, turn (fourth street), river (fifth street), and showdown.

PRE-FLOP. After the dealer has passed out two cards to everyone, players look at their cards. The player to the left of the right blind has the option to fold, call, or raise the previous bet. Play then proceeds clockwise around the table. (For betting and scoring, see Seven-Card Stud.)

FLOP. At the start of the flop round, the dealer places three community cards face up in the middle of the table. Normal play then proceeds, starting with whichever active player is seated to the left of the dealer. That player can either fold or place a bet.

TURN/FOURTH STREET. At the start of the turn round, or fourth street, the dealer places a fourth card face up with the three community cards turned over in the flop. Normal play then proceeds, starting with whichever active player is seated to the left of the dealer. That player can either fold or place a bet.

RIVER/FIFTH STREET. At the start of the river round, the dealer places a fifth and final card in the community pool. Normal play then proceeds, starting with whichever active player is seated to the left of the dealer. That player can either fold or place a bet.

SHOWDOWN. If there are still players in the game after the river round, these players must turn over their cards for all to see. The highest-ranking five-card poker hand takes the pot.

At the end of the round, the dealer, the left blind, and the right blind rotate clockwise, and gameplay begins again.

VARIATIONS

DOUBLE-BOARD HOLD 'EM. Double-Board Hold 'Em has the same general rules and procedures as Texas Hold 'Em, but as the name implies, there are two separate boards of community cards. The same dealing procedures apply for these boards (i.e., during the flop, the dealer reveals three cards for each board and then one card for each board at the end of every round thereafter). The two boards share one pot. If a player has the best hand for one board, the player receives half the pot. If their hand is the best for both boards, they receive the full pot.

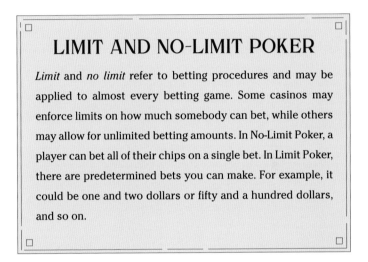

LIMIT AND NO-LIMIT POKER

Limit and *no limit* refer to betting procedures and may be applied to almost every betting game. Some casinos may enforce limits on how much somebody can bet, while others may allow for unlimited betting amounts. In No-Limit Poker, a player can bet all of their chips on a single bet. In Limit Poker, there are predetermined bets you can make. For example, it could be one and two dollars or fifty and a hundred dollars, and so on.

OMAHA HOLD 'EM. In Omaha Hold 'Em, players receive four hole cards instead of two. The game is played as usual to make the best five-card poker hand using two of their own cards and three of the community cards.

PINEAPPLE HOLD 'EM. In Pineapple Hold 'Em, players initially receive three hole cards, but they discard one of their cards before betting begins. Afterward, play proceeds according to traditional Texas Hold 'Em rules.

HISTORY OF TEXAS HOLD 'EM

As the name implies, Texas Hold 'Em originated in the state of Texas. While its specific origins are unclear, the Texas government recognizes Robstown, Texas, as the game's birthplace, dating it to the early twentieth century. During the 1960s, Texas Hold 'Em came to Las Vegas, where it quickly became popular at the Golden Nugget Casino. Before Texas Hold 'Em, a similar game called Draw Poker was played, but it only allowed two bets. Because Texas Hold 'Em allowed for four bets, there was opportunity for bigger winnings and more strategic play. Texas Hold 'Em increased in popularity throughout the late twentieth century. Doyle Brunson's influential 1979 book *Super/System* was the first professional book to discuss Texas Hold 'Em in great detail. In 1988, the court case *Tibbetts v. Van De Kamp* declared that Texas Hold 'Em is legally distinct from Stud Horse and that it is a game of skill.

THIRTY-ONE

Thirty-One, or Scat, is a casino-type card game for two or more players and is played with a standard deck of fifty-two playing cards. In Thirty-One, Aces are worth 11 points, face cards are worth 10 points, and numbered cards are worth their pip (or face) value. The objective of the game is to have a hand that is as close as possible or equal to 31.

SETUP

Before gameplay can begin, a dealer must be selected. Each player draws one card from a shuffled deck. The player with the lowest card becomes the dealer. The dealer shuffles the deck and deals three cards face down to each player one at a time, moving in a clockwise direction. The remaining deck forms the stock, which is placed in the middle of the table. The top card of the stock is flipped over and placed next to the stock, thereby forming the discard pile.

HOW TO PLAY

The player to the left of the dealer begins gameplay. When it is their turn, a player can choose to either pick a card from the stock or pick up the top card from the discard pile. Once a player has chosen a card, they must discard one of their cards, making sure they never have more than three cards in their hand at the end of the turn. All cards are drawn in an attempt to get a hand as close as possible or equal to 31.

Only cards of the same suit count as points. For example, if a player holds an Ace of spades, an 8 of spades, and a King of hearts in their hand, that player's hand is worth 19.

If every card in a player's hand is from a different suit, the highest-valued card becomes the value of the hand. For example, if a player holds an Ace of spades, a Jack of hearts, and a 7 of clubs, the value of the player's hand is 11.

If a player has a three of a kind in any card rank, their hand is worth 30 points.

When a player is comfortable with their hand, they knock on the table. All other players then have one more draw to try to improve their hand. The player with the lowest hand loses that round. If the player who knocks has the lowest hand, they count the loss as two rounds rather than one. When a player loses four rounds, they are out of the game. The last player standing wins the game, and normally, a monetary prize is made from the players' contributions. Typically, whoever loses the round pays a predetermined amount into the pot. The last player standing wins.

HISTORY OF THIRTY-ONE

Thirty-One is one of the card world's oldest games, dating back to the fifteenth century. Considered a gentleman's gambling game, Thirty-One was mentioned in one of St. Bernardine of Siena's anti-gambling sermons, which were given in Italy in the 1400s. Many games scholars consider Thirty-One to be an early ancestor of the games Blackjack and Cribbage.

PLAYING CARDS AND
TAROT CARDS

You'll often come across the claim that our modern deck of playing cards was developed from the tarot deck. Occultists and fortune-tellers like to make the suggestion that tarot decks are in fact the true and original form of playing cards, and that the symbolism of tarot cards lies at the heart of our modern deck.

Some even defend the view that the tarot deck represents a deck that was used by secret societies like the Masons or Knights Templar to transmit sensitive information. According to this interpretation, there are hidden meanings within tarot cards that go back to books and playing cards from ancient times, pre-dating standard playing cards.

In reality, tarot cards appear to have had a separate and much later origin than regular playing cards. It is thought that they may have been created as a means of instruction and education, and it seems doubtful that the earliest tarot cards were created as a result of an interest in the occult or as a means of performing fortune-telling. In fact, the earliest surviving tarot cards date from a period much later than regular playing cards, and the historical evidence supports their original use as additional trump cards. These early tarot cards consisted of twenty-two separate designs with allegorical illustrations that were added to a standard deck, in order to create a larger overall deck that was originally used for gaming. As such, early tarot cards were initially part of a seventy-eight-card deck that was primarily used for more elaborate and complex games that couldn't be played using a standard deck of fifty-two cards.

The symbolism and significance of the original illustrations from the era has been lost and likely simply reflects fifteenth-century cultural fashions in Renaissance Italy. This means that present-day interpretations of these cards don't have an early historical basis.

Tarot cards were used for cartomancy for the first time around 1750, which is more than a couple of centuries after the expanded tarot deck was first conceived and used for gameplay. Fortune-telling with tarot cards only became widely popularized in the latter half of the eighteenth century, and the colorful images of the tarot cards lent themselves especially well to this purpose. Etteilla (a deliberate reversal of the actual surname of Jean-Baptiste Alliette, to make it appear more mystical) was one of the first and most influential fortune-tellers of the time and is considered to be the first professional tarot occultist to make a living by card divination. He claimed that tarot cards were linked to ancient Egypt, and he assigned esoteric meanings to them, many of which are still used today. Antoine Court, a French Mason in the late eighteenth century, made similar claims that tarot cards were derived from the occultic *Book of Thoth*, which supposedly originated in ancient Egypt. It was the source of all knowledge, and was written by the Egyptian god of writing.

Studying it was claimed to reveal secrets about humanity and keys to ancient knowledge.

Many modern day practitioners of the occult and voodoo continue to perpetuate the belief that the tarot is embedded with secret symbols and images that hail back to ancient times, and that tarot can provide answers, direction, and spiritual guidance.

Arthur Edward Waite's approach to the tarot deck at the start of the twentieth century would influence all subsequent tarot playing cards. He was a member of an occultic society called the Hermetic Order of the Golden Dawn, and the designs of the Rider-Waite Tarot deck, which was first published in 1909, became in many ways a standard of the time.

The English occultist Aleister Crowley's deck was painted over several years (1938–1943) and was also very influential; it deliberately included many occultic elements, and some even find it disturbing.

Modern Tarot decks consist of seventy-eight cards with two distinct parts. The Major Arcana (greater secrets) correspond to the original number of twenty-two trump cards, and they are numbered with Roman numerals from I to XXI, along with a Fool card. The Minor Arcana (lesser secrets) consist of fifty-six cards in four suits that are similar to the Italian swords, clubs, coins, and cups, although the clubs are typically called wands, rods, or staves, while the coins are typically called pentacles or disks. Each suit has fourteen cards, with four court cards accompanying ten number cards: King, Queen, Knight, and Page.

Despite claims that tarot is a tool used to uncover the secrets of both the past and the future, it seems most likely that the tarot is not a mystical key to the past, but rather that layers of meaning have been ascribed to it over time. Serious historians remain convinced that tarot's origins lie in an innocent card game, and that occultists have imbued it with a far greater significance than it ever had to begin with, adding meanings that were not present when the artists from the Renaissance painted the first Tarot cards. Academics like Michael Dummett have done extensive research on this topic and make a compelling case that the Tarot deck originated as a popular trick-taking game in fifteenth-century Italy, and that occultic interpretations were unknown prior to the eighteenth century. Even so, tarot decks are still extremely popular today. If nothing else, they give artists and creative designers a larger canvas of cards to work with, resulting in some very artistic and beautifully designed decks.

GLOSSARY

Most specialized hobbies and interests have their own terminology, and the world of playing cards and card games is no different. Most readers likely have some experience with playing cards and with card games, and so you are probably already familiar with quite a few common terms and words that are used. But are you sure that you're using the right words? It's easy to learn new words from other people, but that doesn't guarantee you're thinking of the right meaning.

Is there a difference, for example, between a court card, a picture card, and a face card? What exactly is meant by a spot card, and are there alternative words that are more commonly used for the same thing? What are the proper names for the four suits, and should we have a preference for *clovers* or *clubs*? Could you explain the difference between a hand and a trick, and distinguish between the stock and a tableau?

If you're already an established card connoisseur, this glossary will help give you a quick refresher course and polish your existing knowledge. And if you're still quite new to playing cards, this list will hopefully help you become more informed. Whatever the case, knowing a thing or two about the language of playing cards will help you enjoy them all the more.

These terms relate to playing cards themselves, with common words and phrases relating to how they are made and what they look like.

Many individual card games have their own terms, such as Euchre (bower, going alone, order up, march), Cribbage (crib, go, his heels, his nob, muggins, peg, starter), and Poker (blind, check, hole card, straight), so this is not an exhaustive list, but it focuses on terms that are common to most card games.

Ace—The number 1 card of each suit.

Ace high (or low)—The Ace is the highest (or lowest) ranked card in a suit.

Announce—Name a trump suit or show your melds.

Ante—A bet or contribution to the pot made before the deal.

Auction—The period of bidding before cards are played, to establish the conditions of the game (e.g., the trump suit, how many tricks are needed to win).

Bank—The dealer or house in a gambling game.

Bid—A proposal to win a specific number of tricks or points.

Bidder—Any player who makes a bid, or the player who makes the highest bet.

Black Lady—The Queen of spades, also called the Black Maria.

Blank suit—Having no cards of a specific suit, sometimes also referred to as void.

Blocked—A card that is partially or completely covered by another card, and thus not available to be played or transferred in the layout.

Bluff—Pretend you have better or different cards than what you actually have in hand.

Bridge—A classy flourish where two interwoven halves of a deck spring together, performed during shuffling.

Bridge size—A narrow playing card with a width of 2.25 inches, in contrast to the more common 2.5-inch-wide "poker size."

Burn—Reveal and then bury a card.

Bury—Place a card at the bottom of the deck, or in the middle of the deck, so it can't be easily located

Buy—Draw from the stock or widow.

Carte blanche—A hand with no court cards (but may contain an Ace), also called a blank.

Catch—Getting valuable cards when drawing from the stock or widow.

Chicane—A dealt hand that has no trumps.

Chip—A token or gaming counter used in gambling games in place of money.

Clubs—English term for the French suit trefle, corresponding to swords (Italian/Spanish) and acorns (Swiss/German).

Coffee housing—Acting or speaking in a way to mislead your opponents about the cards you have in hand.

Color—Spades and clubs are black, while hearts and diamonds are red.

Column—Cards in a vertical line extending toward you, where the cards may overlap but show their indices, usually in a tableau.

Combination—A set of cards recognized by the game rules as having a scoring value, usually a set of the same rank or suit.

Contract—Obligation to win a certain number of tricks or points.

Court cards—Kings, Queens, and Jacks. Also called face cards or picture cards.

Cover—Playing a card higher than the previous highest card in a trick.

Cut—Divide the deck into two packets and reverse their order.

Cutthroat—A variant of a partnership game where players play for themselves against the other players.

Deal—Pass out cards to the other players. In card games this is usually done from a face-down pack in clockwise order, starting with the player on the dealer's left.

Dealer—The person who deals cards to the other players.

Deck—A pack of playing cards, usually fifty-two cards plus two Jokers.

Declare—Announce the contract or conditions of play (e.g., name a trump suit or the number of tricks to be won). Alternatively, this can mean to show and score the valid combinations (e.g., melds) of cards in your hand.

Deuce—A card with two pips.

Diamonds—English term for the French suit carreau, corresponding to coins (Italian/Spanish) and bells (Swiss/German).

Discard—Putting an unwanted card in the discard pile, sometimes called "throwing off" when used to refer to playing a worthless card in a trick.

Discard pile—The cards that have been discarded during play, usually face up.

Draw—Take an additional card, usually from the draw pile or stock, and sometimes from the top of the discard pile.

Draw pile—The cards remaining after the deal; also called the "stock."

Dribble—Releasing a deck of cards one at a time from the fingers and thumb so that they fall downward in a steady flow.

Eldest hand—The player next to the dealer (usually on their left) who receives cards first and plays first; sometimes also called first hand.

Exchange—Trade a number of cards from your hand with another player, or draw from the stock and discard the same number (or in the opposite order).

Exit—Force another player to win a trick so as to get out of being the player who leads.

Face cards—Kings, Queens, and Jacks. Also called court cards or picture cards.

Face down—A card placement where its back is showing and its face is adjacent to the table.

Face up—A card placement where its number or picture is showing.

Fan—A spread of cards held in a semicircular shape, with overlapping cards that show the indices.

Faro—A shuffling method where the two halves of the deck interweave perfectly one card at a time, like a zipper.

Finesse—Holding back a certain winning card and playing a card of lesser strength in the hope of capturing an extra trick.

Flash—Expose a card accidentally while dealing or handling a deck.

Flip—Turn a card face up.

Flourish—A visually impressive display of skill performed with playing cards.

Flush—A hand of cards of the same suit.

Fold—Drop out, usually by turning down your face-up cards.

Follow suit—Play a card of the same suit as the first card played.

Force—Making a spectator select a predetermined card apparently at random.

Four of a kind—Four cards of the same rank (e.g., four tens). In some games, this is called a book.

Full house—A combination of five cards that includes three of a kind and a pair.

Go out—Play your last card, thus getting rid of all cards in your hand.

Hand—Cards dealt or held by a player during a game. Also, the portion of a game from when the cards are dealt until they are all played.

Hearts—English term for the French suit coeur, corresponding to cups (Italian/Spanish), flowers (Swiss), and hearts (German).

Honors—The high cards of a suit (Ace, King, Queen, and Jack, and sometimes also the 10), especially if they have scoring value.

In sequence—A requirement that cards be placed on one another exactly one higher (or lower).

Index—The small number/letter and suit symbol in the corner of a card that shows its suit and value, especially useful in a fanned hand.

Joker—Extra card that comes with a fifty-two-card deck; used in some games as a wild card or as the highest trump.

Knave—The Jack of a suit.

Knock—Indicating that all your cards are melded (e.g., in Rummy) or that you won't make a further bet (e.g., in Poker).

Lead—Play the first card of a trick; also, a reference to this card.

Maker—The player who names the trump suit.

Marked—A deck that has secret marks integrated into the artwork on the back of the cards, often enabling the suit and rank of the card to be identified.

Marriage—King and Queen of a suit.

Master card—The highest-ranked card in a suit that is live or unplayed.

Meld—A matched set of three or more cards having the same rank, or having the same suit and being in consecutive order. As a verb, *meld* means to declare or lay out one or more such sets. This term is mainly used in Rummy.

No trump—A declaration where the hand is played with no trump suit.

Numerals—Number cards, as opposed to court cards, also called pip cards or spot cards.

One eyes—The Jack of spades, Jack of hearts, and King of diamonds.

One way—A back design that isn't symmetrical, enabling cards that are upside down to be easily identified.

Outjog—Push out a card from a deck so that its top half is protruding and visible above the other cards.

Overhand—A shuffling method where the cards are moved in sideways packets; the most common method of shuffling cards.

Pack—A deck of playing cards, usually fifty-two cards plus two Jokers.

Packet—Part of a deck, usually consisting of a number of individual cards.

Pair—Two cards of the same rank.

Partnership—Two or more players working together to win.

Pass—Declare that you don't bid or bet, or that you withdraw from the current deal.

Pasteboards—Another term for playing cards, originating from when the front and back of a card were literally pasted together.

Picture cards—Kings, Queens, and Jacks. Also called court cards or face cards.

Pip—The large suit symbols on a card (spade, club, heart, or diamond).

Pip value—The numerical value of a card.

Plain card—A non-trump card; also called plain suit.

Play—Take a card from your hand and use it in a game.

Poker size—A standard-size playing card with a width of 2.5 inches, in contrast to the narrow 2.25-inch-wide bridge size.

Pot—The money or chips representing a game's bets; also called a kitty or pool.

Raise—Increase a preceding bet.

Rank—The ordinal position (number value) of a card in a suit—e.g., 2 of diamonds and 2 of clubs have the same rank, while a King outranks a Queen. This is sometimes also called denomination.

Redeal—Use the cards from the discard pile after the initial stock has been used.

Renege—A failure to play a required card, usually when you don't follow suit; also called revoke.

Renounce—Play a card other than the suit led.

Round—When all players participate once in a deal, bet, or play of a card.

Rubber—A set of three successive games; usually so described in matches of Whist or Bridge.

Ruff—Play a trump in a trick led with a plain suit.

Run—A sequence of two or more cards of adjacent rank, which in some games must be of the same suit; also simply called a sequence.

Sandbagging—The strategy of holding back cards in a good hand to trap an opponent into a greater loss later in the hand.

Sequence—A run of two or more cards of adjacent rank, which in some games must be of the same suit; also called a run.

Shedding—Games where the aim is to be the first player to get rid of all their cards.

Shuffle—Randomize the cards in a deck by a mixing process.

Singleton—Holding one card of any suit.

Spades—English term for the French suit pique, corresponding to batons (Italian), clubs (Spanish), escutcheons (Swiss), and leaves (German).

Spot card—Any card from 2 through 10; also called pip cards, as opposed to court cards.

Spread—Showing a hand, packet, or deck of cards face up, often with cards overlapping.

Stack—Cards placed on each other so only the top card is visible.

Stacked deck—A deck where the cards are set up with a prearranged order.

Stock—The cards remaining after the deal; also called the draw pile.

Suicide King—King of Hearts, so named because of the traditional orientation of the sword he usually holds.

Tableau—The part of a game layout, excluding the foundation, in which cards are arranged and built upon one another. This term is typically used in Solitaire, but can also be used colloquially to refer to any game layout.

Talon—A stack of undealt cards.

Three of a kind—Three cards of the same rank (e.g., three 10s); also called a triplet.

Tops—Highest cards in a suit.

Trey—A card with three pips.

Trick—One card from each player, usually won and taken by the player who played the highest or best card.

Trick taking—Games based on the principle of trick play.

Trump—A selected suit that outranks the other suits (e.g., a 2 of a trump suit will beat a King of any other suit). As a verb, *trump* means to play a trump card that beats other non-trump cards.

Tuck—Short form for *tuck box*, which is the box or case containing the deck.

Turn—In rotation, a player's opportunity to deal, declare, bet, or play.

Turn up—A card placed face up after the deal, to determine (or propose) the trump suit.

Unload—Get rid of the dangerous cards from your hand.

Void—Having no cards of a specific suit, sometimes also referred to as blank suit. As a verb, *void* means the act of discarding all cards of a suit to achieve this.

Waive—Being able to lift a card and play the card below it.

Waste talon—Cards turned up from the stock or hand and laid aside in one or more packets as unwanted or unplayable; sometimes also called a waste or waste pile.

Widow—Extra cards that are dealt face down at the start of the game and don't belong to a particular player; often a player is given an opportunity to exchange some cards with the widow pile.

Wild card—A card that can be used to represent the rank and suit of any other card (as allowed by the game rules), usually as designated by its holder.

Wrapping—Allowing a sequence where an Ace can continue from a King (or even a King and a 2 at the same time); also called building around the corner.

Youngest hand—The player last in turn to bid or play (in contrast to the eldest hand). In two-player games, this is the dealer, who is sometimes also called a pone.

INDEX OF GAMES BY DIFFICULTY

INDEX OF GAMES BY NUMBER OF PLAYERS

IMAGE CREDITS

ix: ©United States Playing Card Company

xi: (Top) "Ladies of a Mandarin Family at Cards" via Wikimedia Commons; (Bottom) Image courtesy of Worshipful Company of Makers of Playing Cards

xv: Image courtesy of Paul Bostock

xvi: Image courtesy of Paul Bostock

xix: Image courtesy of Paul Bostock

xx: 1865 Samuel Hart Poker Deck reproduced by permission of U.S. Gaming Systems, Inc., Stamford, CT., 06902. © U.S. Games Systems, Inc. All Rights Reserved.

3: ©United States Playing Card Company

13: Image courtesy of Cococo Games

14: Painting by Anthony Van Dyck; image via Wikimedia Commons

54: ©United States Playing Card Company

57: Airplane Spotter Playing Cards reproduced by permission of U.S. Games Systems, Inc., Stamford, C., 06902. ©U.S. Games Systems, Inc. All Rights Reserved.

91: Image courtesy of Paul Bostock

92: ©United States Playing Card Company

119: Image courtesy of Midnight Cards

173: Image courtesy of Bona fide Playing Cards

198: ©United States Playing Card Company

216: Rider-Waite Tarot Deck®, known also as the Rider Tarot and the Waite Tarot, reproduced by permission of U.S. Games Systems, Inc., Stamford, CT 06902. ©1971 by U.S. Games Systems, Inc. Further reproduction prohibited. The Rider-Waite Tarot Deck® is a registered trademark of U.S. Games Systems, Inc.

ABOUT THE AUTHOR

Will Roya is a lifelong playing card enthusiast and the founder of PlayingCardDecks.com. He lives in Henderson, Nevada, with his wife, two children, and dog.

PlayingCardDecks.com
🅞 **playingcarddecks_com**   🅕 **@PlayingCardDecks**   ▶ **PlayingCardDecks**